Volume equivalents

IMPERIAL	METRIC	IMPERIAL	METRIC
1fl oz	30ml	15fl oz	450ml
2fl oz	60ml	16fl oz	500ml
2$\frac{1}{2}$fl oz	75ml	1 pint	600ml
3$\frac{1}{2}$fl oz	100ml	1$\frac{1}{4}$ pints	750ml
4fl oz	120ml	1$\frac{1}{2}$ pints	900ml
5fl oz ($\frac{1}{4}$ pint)	150ml	1$\frac{3}{4}$ pints	1 liter
6fl oz	175ml	2 pints	1.2 liters
7fl oz ($\frac{1}{3}$ pint)	200ml	2$\frac{1}{2}$ pints	1.4 liters
8fl oz	240ml	2$\frac{3}{4}$ pints	1.5 liters
10fl oz ($\frac{1}{2}$ pint)	300ml	3 pints	1.7 liters
12fl oz	350ml	3$\frac{1}{2}$ pints	2 liters
14fl oz	400ml	5$\frac{1}{4}$ pints	3 liters

Weight equivalents

IMPERIAL	METRIC	IMPERIAL	METRIC
$\frac{1}{2}$oz	15g	5$\frac{1}{2}$oz	150g
$\frac{3}{4}$oz	20g	6oz	175g
scant 1oz	25g	7oz	200g
1oz	30g	8oz	225g
1$\frac{1}{2}$oz	45g	9oz	250g
1$\frac{3}{4}$oz	50g	10oz	300g
2oz	60g	1lb	450g
2$\frac{1}{2}$oz	75g	1lb 2oz	500g
3oz	85g	1$\frac{1}{2}$lb	675g
3$\frac{1}{2}$oz	100g	2lb	900g
4oz	115g	2$\frac{1}{4}$lb	1kg
4$\frac{1}{2}$oz	125g	3lb 3oz	1.5kg
5oz	140g	4lb	1.8kg

everyday
easy
Cheap
Eats

Based on content previously published
in *The Illustrated Kitchen Bible*
and *The Illustrated Quick Cook*

everyday easy
Cheap Eats

casseroles • stir-fries • savory tarts • sweet treats

LONDON, NEW YORK, MELBOURNE,
MUNICH, AND DELHI

US Editor
Rebecca Warren

Designer
Elma Aquino

Editorial Assistant
Shashwati Tia Sarkar

Senior Jacket Creative
Nicola Powling

Managing Editors
Dawn Henderson, Angela Wilkes

Managing Art Editor
Christine Keilty

Production Editor
Maria Elia

Production Controller
Hema Gohil

Creative Technical Support
Sonia Charbonnier

DK INDIA

Head of Publishing
Aparna Sharma

Editors
Dipali Singh, Saloni Talwar

Designer
Devika Dwarkadas

DTP Coordinator
Sunil Sharma

DTP Designer
Tarun Sharma

Material first published in *The Illustrated Kitchen Bible*, 2008
and *The Illustrated Quick Cook*, 2009
This edition first published in the United States in 2010
by DK Publishing, 375 Hudson Street
New York, New York 10014

10 11 12 13 14 10 9 8 7 6 5 4 3 2 1
177767—May 2010

A catalog record for this book is available
from the Library of Congress.

ISBN 978-0-7566-6192-2

DK books are available at special discounts when purchased in bulk for
sales promotions, premiums, fund-raising or educational use. For details,
contact: DK Publishing Special Markets, 375 Hudson Street, New York,
New York 10014 or SpecialSales@dk.com

Color reproduction by MDP, Bath
Printed and bound in Singapore by Star Standard

Discover more at
www.dk.com

CONTENTS

Being economical in the kitchen doesn't mean that you or your family need to go without good food. On the contrary, everyday recipes should be delicious and satisfying but not leave you out of pocket. This practicality is not new: in every part of the world, the most beloved traditional foods, such as Russian Borscht, Hungarian Goulash, Mexican Quesadillas, and Italian Lasagna, are inexpensive to make for this very reason. Traditional recipes are therefore featured often in this book. These are dishes that you can reproduce reliably day after day, and they have an undeniable feel-good factor.

You can make your food go further by using the advice in the Useful Information section. Planning your meals is the smart way to be frugal—by **Using Leftovers** effectively you can make one meal and use it in different ways over a few days. Try the Quick Fish Pie or Pork and Spring Greens recipes for some tasty ideas. **Batching and Freezing** is another way to maximize your ingredients and minimize wastage. When cooking in large quantities, freeze a batch for later—this is an excellent solution for busy weeknights when you have little time to cook. Many recipes in this book are ideal for batch cooking: try the Sweetcorn Chowder or Provençal Lamb.

Following this is a range of **Recipe Planners** that showcase recipes by themes such as Comfort, Healthy, and Vegetarian so you can easily find something that takes your fancy. For cooks in a hurry, the Quick recipes planner is the first place to look for inspiration.

A selection of step-by-step **Techniques** at the beginning of relevant chapters will refine your core cookery skills. Some techniques will save you time in the kitchen and ensure you get the most from your ingredients, whether you are peeling garlic or coring apples. Other techniques will help you achieve perfect results from your recipe, for example when you need a flavorful stock or faultless pastry.

Recipes in the **Soups and Sandwiches** section are ideal for lunches, light snacks, or to start off a meal. Nothing is better than a warming soup on a cold day: Chorizo and Tomato Soup, Spiced Butternut Squash Soup, and Scotch Broth are all soul-soothing delights. Kids will love the classic sandwich Tuna Melt and spicy Mexican Tacos are the perfect weeknight family supper.

Big, hearty **Casseroles and Bakes** are slow-cooked to get sensational flavor from simple ingredients. They are wonderfully easy to make, too—prepare the ingredients, put them in a casserole or baking dish, then get on with something else (or put your feet up!) while your meal bubbles away in the oven or on the stove. Satisfying dishes such as Chicken with Cider and Cream and Sausage and Mustard Casserole are guaranteed crowd-pleasers.

When you're pushed for time, the **Stir-fries** section will give you plenty of ideas for quick meals. Whether you're looking for an elegant supper of Crispy Rice Noodles with Beef or the perfect breakfast of Parsi Eggs, stir-fries are affordable meals that are ultra-convenient. These one-pot wonders won't leave many dishes to be done either!

Fantastically versatile, great for any occasion, and much easier to make than you might think, **Pies and Tarts** are very rewarding to bake. In this section you'll find everything from exotic Empanadas to homely Sausage and Tomato Pie—eat hot or cold, indoors or outdoors.

After making all the savings on your shopping bill, you'll deserve something from the **Desserts** section. Old-fashioned family favorites such as Bread and Butter Pudding, Plum Crumble, and Baked Jam Roll are brilliant comfort foods that are kind to the wallet.

Home cooking is the best way to enjoy great food on a budget. Give all of these recipes a try and see just how easy it is to do every day.

Using leftovers

Cooking one dish one day and enjoying it in different ways in the days to come is a clever way to plan your weekly meals. Using leftover vegetables and meat in new and creative ways is not only thrifty, but also a great time-saver.

LEFTOVER		NEW DISH
	VEGETABLES **Store** cooked root vegetables in a rigid airtight plastic container. Don't overpack, as they can go soggy. Leave to cool before sealing. Store greens in a covered bowl or rigid plastic container. Leave to cool before covering or sealing. **Refrigerate** cooked vegetables and greens for 1–2 days. **Freeze** leftover root vegetables that have been slightly undercooked. Keep for up to 1 month.	Root vegetables can be turned into bakes, pasta sauces, and frittatas. Leftover greens can be added to casseroles, lasagna, and soups. Alternatively, just reheat greens in a little olive oil, and toss in lemon juice and chilli oil. Serve with some fresh crusty bread.
	POULTRY **Store** the meat and carcass separately, wrapped in plastic wrap, then foil. Refrigerate within 2 hours after it has been cooked. Keep away from uncooked meats. Leftover stuffing and gravy should be stored separately in airtight containers. **Refrigerate** the meat and carcass for 2–3 days; use leftover gravy within 2 days. **Freeze** for up to 3 months. Defrost completely before use.	Chicken bones and meat can be used to prepare stock. Leftover poultry can be added to soups, warm salads, and noodle dishes. Alternatively, use it to make a pasta bake or a fragrant pilaf. Remember to reheat leftover poultry till it is piping hot.
	MEAT **Store** beef, lamb, and pork away from uncooked meats. Refrigerate within 2 hours after it has been cooked. Leftover gravy can be stored in a plastic container. **Refrigerate** meat for 1–3 days; use leftover gravy within 2 days. **Freeze** for up to 3 months. Defrost completely before use.	Leftover meat can be added to casseroles, stir-fries, bakes, and pies. Alternatively, use it in casseroles and pasta bakes. Minced, it can be made into pies such as Shepherd's Pie. Remember to reheat leftover meat till it is piping hot.
	FISH **Store** in a shallow rigid plastic container and seal, or put on a plate and wrap well with plastic wrap. Store away from uncooked foods. Refrigerate within 2 hours after it has been cooked. **Refrigerate** for 1–2 days. **Freeze** for up to 3 months. Defrost completely before use.	Leftover fish can be added to salads, pastas, and pies. You can also use it to make fish cakes. Remember to reheat leftover fish till it is piping hot.

Batch and freeze

Make-ahead dishes for the freezer save you time and effort. To use them, thaw them slowly overnight in the refrigerator; it is not only the safest way to defrost, but also the best way to retain the food's flavor and texture.

FOOD		PACKAGING	STORAGE	DEFROST
	SOUPS Once cooked, leave to cool completely, then pack into 16fl oz (500ml) portions. Don't freeze in over-large portions, as defrosting will take too long.	Pack in sealable freezer bags or plastic containers. Spoon stock into ice cube trays and freeze. Once frozen, remove from tray and transfer to a freezer bag and seal.	Soups for up to 3 months. Stocks for up to 6 months.	Thaw overnight in the refrigerator, then reheat in a pan until piping hot, or heat in the microwave on High for a few minutes.
	STEWS Foods with a very high fat content will go rancid after a couple of months in the freezer, so choose lean cuts of meat. Cool completely before freezing.	Freeze in sealable freezer bags or foil containers, or ladle into rigid sealable plastic containers. Make sure meat is well covered with liquid, otherwise it will dry out.	Up to 3 months.	Thaw overnight in the refrigerator, then reheat in a pan, or in the oven at 350°F (180°C), for about 30 minutes, or until piping hot, or heat in the microwave on High for a few minutes.
	PIES Baking is the ideal time to batch cook. You can freeze pastry cooked or uncooked. Cool completely before freezing.	**Uncooked:** Freeze blocks of pastry layered with wax paper, then wrapped in plastic wrap. **Cooked:** Freeze pastry cases and pies wrapped in a double layer of plastic wrap.	Uncooked pies and pastry for up to 3 months. Cooked pies and pastry cases for up to 6 months.	Bake uncooked pastries from frozen at 400°F (200°C), for 15 minutes. Thaw cooked pies overnight, then bake at 350°F (180°C) for 30 minutes, or until piping hot.

A guide to symbols

The recipes in this book are accompanied by symbols that alert you to important information.

 Tells you how many people the recipe serves, or how much is produced.

 Indicates how much time you will need to prepare and cook a dish. Next to this symbol you will also find out if additional time is required for such things as marinating, standing, or cooling. Read the recipe to find out exactly how much extra time to allow.

 Points out a healthy dish—low in fat or low GI (Glycemic Index).

This is especially important, as it alerts you to what has to be done before you can begin to cook the recipe, or to parts of the recipe that may take a long time to complete.

This denotes that special equipment is required, such as a deep-fat fryer or skewers. Where possible, alternatives are given.

This symbol accompanies freezing information.

Healthy

Chicken stir-fried with spring onion, basil, and lemon grass page 122

Spicy garlic green vegetable medley page 108

Aduki bean stew page 82

Smoked fish and anchovy gratin page 94

Ribollita page 64

Chicken with noodles and basil page 118

Pork and spring greens page 110

Baby zucchini with fish and couscous page 104

Spiced bean and herb hash page 102

Asian turkey and noodle soup page 50

Chickpea and vegetable stew page 90

Hungarian goulash page 78

Zucchini, herb, and lemon tagine page 70

Quick—Savory

Tuna melt page 42

Chickpeas with spinach page 120

Fried mozzarella panini
page 34

Reuben sandwich page 60

Chorizo with peppers page 130

Quick fish pie page 86

Quesadillas with ham, gherkin, and smoked cheese page 62

Quick—Sweet

Bananas flambéed with Calvados page 204

Hot chocolate cakes page 194

Lemon and sugar crêpes page 212

Pear gratin page 206

Semolina page 200

Sticky toffee and banana pudding page 196

Kaiserschmarrn page 208

Vegetarian

Feta filo pie page 180

Chickpea and vegetable stew page 90

Sweet corn chowder page 36

Fried mozzarella panini page 34

Gruyère tart page 160

Leek and cheese tart page 174

Cauliflower soup page 38

Aduki bean stew page 82

Chickpeas with spinach
page 120

Parmesan cheese and walnut tart page 164

Spicy garlic green vegetable medley page 108

Vichyssoise page 44

Quesadillas with salsa Mexicana page 48

Spiced butternut squash soup
page 46

Cheesy spinach squares
page 154

Spiced bean and herb hash
page 102

Light bites

Vegetable samosas page 146

Chorizo with peppers page 130

Pan bagnat page 52

Goat cheese tartlets page 142

Quesasdillas with salsa Mexicana page 48

Feta and pumpkin pastries page 156

Croque monsieur page 57

Cheese and pepper jalousie page 176

Patatas bravas page 128

Empanadas page 150

Parsi eggs page 116

Sweet corn and pepper filo triangles page 179

19

Comfort—Savory

Tomato and chorizo soup page 40

Chicken with cider and cream page 80

Sweet corn chowder page 36

Steak and ale pie page 168

Borscht page 32

Sausage and mustard casserole page 100

Pork and bean stew page 76

Chicken with pancetta, peas, and mint page 88

Steak and kidney pudding page 172

Comfort—Sweet

Sticky toffee and banana pudding page 196

Plum crumble page 202

Apple Charlotte page 188

Blueberry cobbler page 186

Baked jam roll page 214

Rice pudding page 198

Make vegetable stock

Simmering water with vegetables will capture their delicate flavor. Use the stock to flavor vegetarian soups, stews, and risottos.

1 Place chopped carrots, celery, onions, and a bouquet garni into a large stockpot. Cover with water and bring to a boil. Reduce the heat and simmer the stock for up to 1 hour.

2 Ladle the stock through a fine sieve, pressing the vegetables against the sieve to extract any extra liquid. Season to taste with salt and pepper, let cool, and refrigerate for up to 3 days.

Make chicken stock

Use homemade chicken stock for soups, stews, and risottos.

1 Add raw chicken bones, or the bones and scraps from a cooked chicken into a large stockpot with carrots, celery, onions, and a bouquet garni. Cover with water and bring to a boil.

2 Reduce the heat and simmer for 2–3 hours, skimming frequently. Ladle the stock through a fine sieve and season to taste. Let cool and refrigerate for up to 3 days.

Make quesadillas

Quesadillas are essentially toasted sandwiches, using tortillas. You can use wheat or corn tortillas, and fill them with cheese and your favorite ingredients.

1 Have all your ingredients ready-prepared—2 tortillas, and your chosen fillings. Here we're using scant 1oz (25g) Gruyère cheese, grated, and a handful of sliced jalapeño chiles from a jar.

2 Heat a frying pan with a little olive oil (you can omit this if you prefer), then place one tortilla in the pan. Add the topping ingredients, leaving a little room around the edge so the cheese doesn't spill out.

3 Lay the other tortilla precisely over the top and press down firmly with a spatula to seal, paying particular attention to the edges. Leave it to warm through for a couple of minutes.

4 Flip the quesadilla over and leave it to cook on the other side for a minute or two. When cooked through, transfer to a plate, and slice into halves or quarters. Serve immediately while hot.

Andalucian soup

A fresh soup from southern Spain, this is similar to gazpacho, the popular chilled Spanish soup.

INGREDIENTS

4oz (115g) day-old rustic bread, crusts removed
3 tbsp olive oil, plus more to garnish
2 tbsp red wine vinegar
4 ripe large tomatoes, skinned and seeded
1 cucumber, peeled, seeded, and chopped
1 red bell pepper, seeded and quartered
1 onion, roughly chopped
3 garlic cloves
salt and freshly ground black pepper
2 hard-boiled eggs, peeled and chopped
2 slices of Serrano ham or prosciutto, cut into thin strips

METHOD

1 Break the bread into pieces and place in a bowl. Add the oil and vinegar, mix well, let stand for about 10 minutes, until softened.

2 Purée the tomatoes, cucumber, red pepper, onion, and garlic with $1/2$ cup water in a blender or food processor. Add the bread and process. Season.

3 Transfer to a bowl and chill at least 30 minutes. Ladle into bowls and top each with hard-boiled eggs, ham, and a drizzle of olive oil. Serve chilled.

4 servings

**prep 15 mins,
plus soaking
and chilling**

**blender or
food processor**

Sopa de tortilla

Fresh lime juice, cilantro, and ancho chiles add an unmistakable Mexican flavor to this tomato soup.

INGREDIENTS

5 tbsp vegetable oil
½ onion, finely chopped
2 large garlic cloves, finely chopped
1lb (450g) ripe tomatoes, skinned and seeded
6 cups chicken or vegetable stock
1 or 2 dried ancho chiles, seeded
2 corn tortillas, cut into strips
3 tbsp chopped cilantro
2 tbsp fresh lime juice
salt and freshly ground black pepper
¾ cup shredded queso fresco or ricotta salata cheese
2 limes, cut into wedges, for serving

METHOD

1 Heat 1 tbsp of the oil in a large saucepan over medium heat. Add the onion and cook, stirring, for 5 minutes, until softened. Add the garlic and stir for 30 seconds. Transfer to a food processor or blender, add the tomatoes, and process until smooth.

2 Return the purée to the pan and simmer for 8–10 minutes, stirring constantly, until reduced by one-third. Stir in the stock and bring to a boil. Reduce the heat, partially cover the pan, and simmer gently for 15 minutes.

3 Place a nonstick frying pan over medium heat. Add the chiles, and press them flat with a spatula until they begin to blister, then turn them and repeat for the other side. Transfer to a plate and cool. Cut into small pieces and set aside.

4 Heat the remaining oil in a frying pan until hot but not smoking. Add the tortilla strips in batches and fry just until crisp. Remove with a slotted spoon, and drain on paper towels.

5 When ready to serve, add the chiles to the soup and bring to a boil. Simmer for 3 minutes, or until the chiles are soft. Stir in the cilantro, lime juice, and salt and pepper to taste. Ladle the soup into bowls, top with the tortillas and cheese, and serve with the limes.

PREPARE AHEAD Steps 1–4 can be prepared up to a day ahead. Store the crisp tortilla strips in an airtight container.

4 servings

prep 15 mins
• cook 50 mins

food processor
or blender

Tacos

Taco shells can be filled with all sorts of spicy fillings and make great party food.

INGREDIENTS

2 tbsp olive oil
1 onion, finely chopped
1 garlic clove, minced
1lb 2oz (500g) ground round
2 tbsp chili powder
1 tsp dried oregano
3 tbsp tomato paste
12 crisp taco shells
iceberg lettuce, shredded, to serve
Cheddar cheese, grated, to serve

METHOD

1 Heat the oil in a frying pan. Add the onion and garlic and cook, stirring, for 3 minutes. Add the beef and brown, about 8 minutes. Drain off fat. Stir in the chili powder and oregano, tomato paste, and ½ cup water. Simmer until thickened, for 10 minutes. Season.

2 Meanwhile, preheat the oven to 300°F (150°C). Bake the shells on a sheet for 4 minutes. Spoon the meat into the shells and top each with shredded lettuce and Cheddar cheese.

GOOD WITH Tomato salsa, jalapeño peppers, and sour cream.

4 servings

**prep 15 mins
• cook 25 mins**

Borscht

This classic Russian soup is thickly textured and satisfying.

INGREDIENTS
2 large beets
1 onion
1 carrot
1 celery stalk
2 tbsp vegetable oil
one 14.5oz (411g) can chopped tomatoes
1 garlic clove, chopped
6 cups vegetable stock
2 bay leaves
4 whole cloves
2 tbsp fresh lemon juice
salt and freshly ground black pepper

METHOD
1 Roughly shred the beets, onion, carrot, and celery.

2 Heat the oil in a large saucepan over medium-low heat. Add the beets, onion, carrot, and celery, and cook, stirring occasionally, for 5 minutes, or until just softened.

3 Stir in the tomatoes with their juices and the garlic. Cook, stirring often, for 2–3 minutes. Stir in the stock and return to a boil.

4 Tie the bay leaves and cloves in a small piece of rinsed cheesecloth. Add to the pot. Reduce the heat to low and cover. Simmer for 1¼ hours.

5 Discard the cheesecloth packet. Stir in the lemon juice and season with salt and pepper. Ladle the soup into warm bowls and serve.

GOOD WITH A garnish of sour cream or grated carrot, and chunks of dark rye bread.

6 servings

prep 15 mins
• cook 1 hr
30 mins

cheesecloth

33

Fried mozzarella panini

Served hot, this truly indulgent snack has a melting center.

INGREDIENTS
8 slices of sourdough bread
2 tbsp olive oil, plus more as needed
$5^{1}/_{2}$oz (150g) thinly sliced mozzarella
12 sun-dried tomatoes, coarsely chopped
16 large basil leaves, torn
salt and freshly ground black pepper

METHOD
1 Preheat the oven to 200°F (95°C). Drizzle the bread on both sides with the oil.

2 Top four bread slices with the mozzarella, tomatoes, and basil. Season with salt and pepper.

3 Top with the remaining bread and compress with your hands, making sure none of the filling is sticking out.

4 Heat a heavy frying pan over high heat. Add 1 tbsp oil and tilt to coat the bottom of the pan. Carefully add 2 sandwiches. Cook, turning once, about 5 minutes, until golden on both sides. Transfer to a baking sheet and keep warm while frying the remaining sandwiches in the remaining oil.

5 Slice each sandwich in half and transfer each to a plate. Serve immediately.

GOOD WITH Arugula leaves drizzled with balsamic vinegar.

4 servings

prep 10 mins
• cook 12 mins

Sweet corn chowder

Full of potatoes and sweet corn, this is a simple but tasty, thick soup.

INGREDIENTS
2 tbsp olive oil
2 onions, finely chopped
salt and freshly ground black pepper
6–8 medium potatoes, peeled,
   and cut into bite-size chunks
two 12oz (350g) cans corn, drained
5 cups hot vegetable stock
handful of parsley, finely chopped
4 tbsp heavy cream (optional), to serve

METHOD
1 Heat the oil in a large saucepan, add the onions, and cook over low heat for 6–8 minutes or until soft. Season with salt and pepper, then stir in the potatoes and cook over low heat for 5 minutes.

2 Mash the corn a little with the back of a fork, then add to the pan. Pour in the stock, bring to a boil, then reduce to a simmer and cook for 15 minutes or until the potatoes are soft. Stir in the parsley and season again with salt and pepper if needed.

3 Stir in the cream (if using), and serve.

PREPARE AHEAD This recipe makes a large quantity so you may want to freeze some. Before adding the cream, let cool completely, transfer to a freezer-proof container, then freeze. To serve, defrost in the refrigerator overnight, then reheat in a pan until piping hot.

8 servings

prep 15 mins
• cook 25 mins

healthy option
(without
the cream)

freeze for up to
3 months

Cauliflower soup

The potatoes and cauliflower give this soup a silky texture.

INGREDIENTS
2 tbsp olive oil
2 onions, finely chopped
salt and freshly ground black pepper
3 garlic cloves, finely chopped
4 celery ribs, finely chopped
2 bay leaves
1½lb (675g) potatoes, cut into bite-sized cubes
15 cups hot vegetable stock
2 cauliflowers, trimmed and cut into florets
drizzle of heavy cream (optional), to serve

METHOD
1 Heat the oil in large pan, add the onions, and cook over low heat for 6–8 minutes or until soft. Season with salt and pepper, then add the garlic, celery, and bay leaves and cook for 5 minutes or until the celery begins to soften. Stir in the potatoes and cook for 5 minutes, then pour in the stock, bring to a boil, and cook for 15 minutes or until the potatoes are nearly soft.

2 Add the cauliflower and cook for 10 minutes or until it is soft but not watery. Remove the bay leaves and discard, then transfer the soup to a food processor or blender and process until smooth. Add a little more hot stock if it seems too thick. Taste and season with salt and pepper as needed. Stir in the heavy cream, if using, and serve.

GOOD WITH Warm crusty rolls and a sprinkling of ground cumin in each bowl to add a warming, spicy flavor.

8 servings

prep 15 mins
• cook 40 mins

healthy option
(without
the cream)

blender or
food processor

Tomato and chorizo soup

Chickpeas add extra substance to the Spanish flavors of this soup.

INGREDIENTS
2 tbsp olive oil
9oz (250g) chorizo, cut into small cubes
2 red onions, finely chopped
4 celery ribs, finely diced
4 carrots, finely diced
3 garlic cloves, finely chopped
salt and freshly ground black pepper
one 28oz (800g) can diced tomatoes
4 cups hot vegetable stock
two 14oz (400g) cans chickpeas, drained
handful of cilantro leaves, finely chopped, to serve

METHOD
1 Heat half the oil in a large heavy-based saucepan, add the chorizo, and cook over medium heat, stirring occasionally, for 5 minutes or until beginning to crisp. Remove and set aside.

2 Heat the remaining oil in the pan, add the onions, and cook over low heat for 6–8 minutes or until soft. Stir in the celery, carrots, and garlic, season with salt and pepper, then cook over low heat, stirring occasionally, for 8 minutes or until tender. Add the tomatoes, stock, and chickpeas and simmer for 15 minutes. Return the chorizo to the pan, then taste and season again with salt and pepper if needed. Stir in the cilantro and serve.

PREPARE AHEAD This recipe makes a large quantity so you may want to freeze some. Before adding the cilantro, let cool completely, transfer to a freezer-proof container, then freeze. To serve, defrost in the refrigerator overnight, then transfer to a pan and heat until piping hot. Stir in some fresh cilantro, and serve.

8 servings

prep 20 mins
• cook 40 mins

freeze for up to 3 months

Tuna melt

This version of the diner classic is enlivened with the tangy flavors of red pepper, lemon, and ketchup.

INGREDIENTS

4 English muffins
1 tbsp olive oil
1 red bell pepper, seeded and finely chopped
4 scallions, white and green parts, thinly sliced
2 shallots, finely chopped
two 6oz (175g) cans albacore tuna, drained
2 tbsp ketchup
6 tbsp mayonnaise
grated zest of 1 lemon
4 large, thin slices of sharp Cheddar cheese, halved diagonally

METHOD

1 Position a broiler rack 6in (15cm) from the heat and preheat. Split the muffins and toast.

2 Heat the oil in a small frying pan over medium heat. Add the red pepper, scallions, and shallots. Cook, stirring often, about 3 minutes. Add the tuna, breaking up the chunks with a fork. Cook for about 1 minute, until the tuna is heated through. Remove the pan from the heat and stir in the ketchup, 2 tbsp of the mayonnaise, and the lemon zest.

3 Spread the remaining mayonnaise over the cut sides of the muffins. Spread 4 muffin halves with the tuna mixture and arrange the cheese triangles on top.

4 Grill until the cheese melts. Top with the remaining 4 muffin halves. Serve at once.

GOOD WITH A selection of your favorite pickles such as pickled cucumbers and sweetcorn relish.

4 servings

prep 15 mins
• cook 10 mins

Vichyssoise

Despite its French name, this silky, smooth chilled soup originates from America.

INGREDIENTS

2 tbsp vegetable oil

3 large leeks, cleaned, white and pale green
   parts only, finely sliced

4¾ cups fresh vegetable stock

1 large baking potato, such as russet or Burbank,
   peeled and chopped

1 celery stalk, roughly chopped

salt and freshly ground black pepper

⅔ cup heavy cream, plus more to garnish

2 tbsp finely chopped chives, to serve

METHOD

1 Heat the oil in a large heavy saucepan over medium heat. Add the leeks and cover. Cook, gently shaking the pot from time to time, for about 15 minutes, or until the leeks are softened and golden.

2 Add the stock, potato, and celery and bring to a boil, stirring often. Season with salt and pepper. Cover, reduce the heat to medium-low, and simmer for 30 minutes, until the vegetables are tender.

3 Remove the pan from the heat and let cool slightly. In batches, purée in a blender with the lid ajar. Season with salt and pepper and cool completely. Stir in the cream. Cover and refrigerate at least 3 hours, or until well chilled.

4 Ladle into soup bowls, sprinkle with chives and pepper, and add a drizzle of cream. Serve chilled.

6 servings

**prep 15 mins,
plus chilling
• cook 30 mins**

**chill for at
least 3 hrs**

blender

Spiced butternut squash soup

You could use any winter squash for this spicy, comforting soup.

INGREDIENTS
2 tbsp olive oil
2 onions, finely chopped
salt and freshly ground black pepper
3 garlic cloves, finely chopped
4 sage leaves, finely chopped
2 red chiles, seeded and finely chopped
pinch of freshly grated nutmeg
1 large butternut squash or 2 small ones, halved, peeled,
   seeded, and chopped into small pieces
2 potatoes, cut into small pieces
5 cups hot vegetable stock
chili oil and grated Gruyère cheese, to serve

METHOD
1 Heat the oil in a large soup pot, add the onions, and cook over low heat for 6–8 minutes or until soft. Season with salt and pepper, then add the garlic, sage, chiles, and nutmeg and cook for a few seconds.

2 Stir in the squash, then add the potatoes and stock. Bring to a boil, reduce to a simmer, and cook for 20–30 minutes or until the squash and potatoes are soft. Transfer to a blender or food processor and process until blended and smooth. Season again with salt and pepper. Serve with a drizzle of chili oil and a sprinkling of Gruyère cheese.

8 servings

prep 20 mins
• cook 40 mins

healthy option

**blender or
food processor**

Quesadillas with salsa Mexicana

Traditionally, quesadillas are deep-fried. This method is a healthier option.

INGREDIENTS
8 flour tortillas
2 cups shredded sharp Cheddar cheese
guacamole, to serve

For the salsa Mexicana
2 large ripe tomatoes, seeded and finely chopped
$\frac{1}{2}$ onion, finely chopped
3 tbsp chopped cilantro
1 green chile, seeded and minced
1 garlic clove, minced
juice of $\frac{1}{2}$ lime
salt

METHOD
1 To make the salsa, combine all the ingredients in a bowl. Season with the salt. Set aside to allow the flavors to blend.

2 Preheat the oven to 200°F (95°C). Heat a heavy frying pan over medium heat. Place 1 tortilla in the pan and heat for 30 seconds. Sprinkle $\frac{1}{2}$ cup of the cheese over the surface. Top with another tortilla and press down lightly with a spatula.

3 Cook, turning once, until the quesadilla is lightly toasted on both sides and the cheese has melted. Transfer to a baking sheet and keep warm in the oven while making the remaining quesadillas. To serve, cut each quesadilla in halves or quarters and serve immediately with the salsa Mexicana and guacamole on the side.

makes 4

prep 10 mins
• cook 20 mins

Asian turkey and noodle soup

A light, fragrant, and restorative broth.

INGREDIENTS
1½ pints (900ml) vegetable stock
2 tbsp soy sauce
1 lemon grass stalk, sliced
one 1in (2.5cm) piece of fresh ginger, peeled and sliced
2 skinless turkey breast fillets, about 7oz (200g) each
10oz (300g) fine rice noodles
1 red chile, deseeded and sliced
handful of cilantro leaves
salt and freshly ground black pepper

METHOD

1 Pour the hot vegetable stock into a large saucepan. Add a generous splash of soy sauce, the lemon grass, ginger, and turkey breast fillets. Bring to a boil, reduce the heat slightly, and simmer for 15–20 minutes, depending on size, until the turkey is fully poached and cooked through. Remove from the pan using a slotted spoon, and shred when cool.

2 Add the rice noodles and red chile to the poaching liquid, and simmer for 5 minutes. If necessary, add boiling water to cover the noodles. Return the shredded turkey to the pan with fresh cilantro leaves and heat through. Season with salt and pepper to taste and serve immediately.

4 servings

prep 10 mins,
plus cooling
• cook 30 mins

healthy option

Pan bagnat

Popular in the area around Nice in the south of France, the name of this traditional worker's sandwich roughly translates as "wet bread".

INGREDIENTS

4 round crusty rolls
2 garlic cloves, cut in half
4 tbsp olive oil
1 tbsp white wine vinegar
salt and freshly ground black pepper
one 6oz (175g) can tuna in oil, drained
$\frac{1}{2}$ green pepper, seeded and sliced
2 scallions, sliced
$\frac{1}{4}$ cucumber, thinly sliced
$\frac{1}{2}$ cup green beans, cooked
8 pitted Kalamata olives
1 hard-boiled egg, sliced
2 large tomatoes, sliced
12 anchovy fillets
8 basil leaves

METHOD

1 Cut each roll in half and pull out most of the soft crumbs. Rub the insides of the rolls with the cut sides of the garlic. Mix the oil and vinegar and season with salt and pepper. Drizzle over the cut surfaces of the rolls.

2 Mix together the tuna, green pepper, scallions, cucumber, green beans, and olives. Divide the tuna mixture among the bottom halves of the rolls. Top each with equal amounts of the sliced egg and tomatoes, then 3 anchovy fillets and 2 basil leaves. Cover with the top of the rolls.

3 Wrap each in plastic wrap and refrigerate for at least 1 hour. Serve chilled or at room temperature.

makes 4

prep 20 mins, plus chilling

Scotch broth

A traditional, stew-like soup, this Scottish dish is extremely filling.

INGREDIENTS

1lb (450g) lamb neck
salt and freshly ground black pepper
2 tbsp olive oil
1 onion, finely chopped
4 carrots, finely chopped
4 celery ribs, finely chopped
2 cups hot chicken stock
8oz (225g) pearl barley
handful of parsley, finely chopped

METHOD

1 Put the lamb in a large saucepan, cover with cold water, and season with salt and pepper. Bring to a boil, then simmer for 30 minutes or until cooked. Remove with a slotted spoon, let cool slightly, then shred and set aside. Reserve the cooking liquid.

2 Heat the oil in a large saucepan, add the onion, and cook over low heat for 5 minutes or until soft. Add the carrots and celery and cook over very low heat for 10 minutes. Strain the reserved liquid, then add to the pan, and pour in the stock. Season with salt and pepper, then add the pearl barley and lamb. Bring to a boil, then reduce to a simmer, and cook over really low heat for 1 hour or until the pearl barley is cooked. Add some hot water if it begins to dry out too much. Stir in the parsley, then taste and season again with salt and pepper if needed, and serve hot.

PREPARE AHEAD This recipe makes a large quantity so you may want to freeze some. Before adding the parsley, let cool completely, transfer to a freezer-proof container, ensuring the lamb is completely covered in liquid, and freeze. To serve, defrost in the refrigerator overnight, then reheat in a pan until piping hot. Stir through the parsley, and serve.

8 servings

prep 20 mins
• cook 1 hr
45 mins

freeze for up to
3 months

Croque monsieur

In France, these toasted cheese and ham sandwiches are a popular snack.

INGREDIENTS

14oz (400g) Gruyère cheese
4 tbsp butter, plus softened butter for spreading
2 tbsp all-purpose flour
²/₃ cup whole milk
2 tsp Dijon mustard
8 slices white sandwich bread
8 thin slices of ham

METHOD

1 Cut 4oz (115g) of the cheese into thin slices and shred the rest.

2 Melt the butter in a medium saucepan over low heat. Whisk in the flour and let bubble without browning for 1 minute. Whisk in the milk. Simmer, whisking often, until smooth and thick. Add the shredded cheese and mustard and stir until the cheese is melted.

3 Position a broiler rack 6in (15cm) from the heat and preheat the broiler. Toast the bread slices on 1 side only. Spread the untoasted sides lightly with butter, then top 4 slices with the ham and sliced cheese. Press the remaining 4 bread slices on top, toasted sides up, and spread with the cheese mixture.

4 Broil about 2 minutes until the sauce is bubbling and golden brown. Slice each croque monsieur on the diagonal and serve at once.

GOOD WITH A green salad and French fries or potato chips.

PREPARE AHEAD Steps 1 and 2 can be completed 1 day ahead but the assembled croque monsieurs must be eaten immediately after toasting.

makes 4

prep 15 mins
• cook 10 mins

White bean soup

This thick soup from northern Italy is guaranteed to keep out the winter chills.

INGREDIENTS

8oz (225g) dried cannellini beans
3 tbsp olive oil
2 onions, finely chopped
2 garlic cloves, minced
5 cups chicken or vegetable stock
1 celery stalk, chopped
3 or 4 parsley stems
1 bay leaf
1 tbsp lemon juice
salt and freshly ground black pepper
2oz (60g) pancetta, chopped (optional)
3 shallots, thinly sliced
3oz (85g) Italian fontina or taleggio

METHOD

1 Soak the beans in cold water to cover overnight. Drain.

2 Heat 2 tbsp of oil in a saucepan over medium-low heat. Add the onions and cook, stirring, for 8 minutes, until translucent. Add the garlic and cook for 1 minute.

3 Add the drained beans, stock, celery, parsley, and bay leaf. Bring to a boil over high heat. Cover and simmer about $1^1/_2$ hours, stirring, or until the beans are very tender. Stir in the lemon juice.

4 Remove the bay leaf. In batches, with the lid ajar, purée the soup in a blender. Return to the pan and season. Keep warm.

5 Heat the remaining oil in a small frying pan over medium heat. Add the pancetta (if using) and cook, stirring, 5 minutes, until browned. Stir in the shallots and cook 3 minutes, until softened.

6 Trim off any rind from and dice the cheese. Stir into the soup. Ladle into bowls, and sprinkle with the pancetta mixture. Serve hot.

4 servings

prep 30 mins, plus soaking • cook 2 hrs

soak the beans overnight to rehydrate them

blender

Reuben sandwich

An all-time favorite of New York delicatessens.

INGREDIENTS
8oz (225g) sauerkraut
8 slices rye bread
$\frac{1}{2}$ cup store-bought Russian salad dressing
12oz (350g) sliced corned beef
4oz (115g) sliced Swiss cheese
4 tbsp butter

METHOD
1 Rinse the sauerkraut in a colander. Place a plate on top and let drain in the sink for 15 minutes.

2 Spread the bread slices with the dressing. Divide the corned beef, Swiss cheese, and sauerkraut over 4 slices. Top each with a bread slice, dressing side down.

3 Melt 1 tbsp of butter in a very large frying pan over medium heat. Add 2 of the sandwiches and top each with a small heat-proof plate. Cook for about 2 minutes, or until the underside is golden brown.

4 Flip the sandwiches over, removing and replacing the plates. Add 1 tbsp of butter and cook another 2 minutes, or until the other side is golden brown. Transfer to a platter and tent with aluminum foil. Repeat with the remaining sandwiches and butter. Serve hot.

GOOD WITH Sour dill pickles.

makes 4

prep 10 mins
• cook 8–12 mins

Quesadillas with ham, gherkin, and smoked cheese

Northern European flavors give this Latin snack an interesting twist.

INGREDIENTS
4 tbsp olive oil
8 wheat or corn tortillas
10oz (300g) smoked cheese
  or sharp Cheddar cheese, grated
1lb 2oz (500g) cooked ham, sliced
8 gherkins, sliced
salt and freshly ground black pepper

METHOD

1 Heat the oil in a nonstick frying pan, then fry one tortilla for 1 minute, or until golden.

2 Sprinkle with $2^{1}/_{2}$oz (75g) of the cheese, leaving a little room around the edge. Top with $4^{1}/_{2}$oz (125g) of the ham and 2 gherkins, then season with salt and pepper.

3 Top with the other tortilla, pressing it down with the back of a spatula to sandwich the two together. Carefully turn it over, and cook the other side for another minute, until golden and the cheese melted. Transfer to a baking sheet and keep warm in the oven while making the remaining quesadillas.

4 Slice each quesadilla in halves or quarters, and serve.

GOOD WITH A tomato salsa or relish.

makes 4

prep 5 mins
• cook 20 mins

Ribollita

This Tuscan soup was traditionally re-boiled (*ribolitta* in Italian) from the day before, giving it its name.

INGREDIENTS

2 tbsp olive oil
2 onions, finely chopped
salt and freshly ground black pepper
4 garlic cloves, finely chopped
4 carrots, finely chopped
8 tomatoes, skinned and roughly chopped
two 14oz (400g) cans drained cannellini beans
1lb (450g) potatoes, cut into bite-sized pieces
12oz (350g) calvo nero or kale, chopped
5 cups hot vegetable stock
1 tbsp rosemary leaves, finely chopped
½ ciabatta, cut into cubes, to serve
drizzle of olive oil, plus extra to serve
freshly grated Parmesan cheese, to serve

METHOD

1 Heat the oil in a saucepan, add the onions, and cook over low heat for 6–8 minutes or until soft. Season with salt and pepper, then stir in the garlic and carrots and cook for 5 minutes.

2 Preheat the oven to 400°F (200°C). Stir in the tomatoes, beans, potatoes, and calvo nero and cook for 5 minutes. Pour in the stock, add the rosemary, and simmer over low heat for 15–20 minutes or until the potatoes are soft. Taste and season again with salt and pepper.

3 Place the ciabatta cubes on a baking sheet, drizzle with olive oil, and bake in the oven for 10 minutes or until golden. Serve the Ribollita topped with the ciabatta, a drizzle of olive oil, and a sprinkling of Parmesan cheese.

PREPARE AHEAD This soup will improve in flavor if made a day ahead; complete steps 1 and 2, cover, and chill. To reheat, transfer to a saucepan and heat until piping hot before serving with the ciabatta croutons and cheese.

8 servings

prep 20 mins
• cook 40 mins

healthy option

freeze for
up to 3 months

Peel and dice an onion

Once an onion is halved, it can be sliced or diced. This technique is for quick dicing, which helps prevent your eyes from watering.

1 Using a sharp chef's knife, cut the onion lengthwise in half and peel off the skin, leaving the root to hold the layers together.

2 Lay one half cut-side down. Make a few slices into the onion horizontally, cutting up to but not through the root.

3 With the tip of your knife, start to slice down through the layers vertically, cutting as close to the root as possible.

4 Cut across the vertical slices to produce even-sized dice. Use the root to hold the onion steady, then discard it when all the onion is diced.

Peel and chop garlic

Garlic is essential to many recipes, and peeling and preparing it is easy once you know how. Before you start, separate the cloves from the bulb.

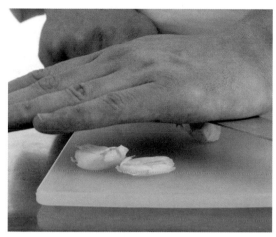

1 Place the garlic clove flat on a cutting board. Place a large knife blade on top and press it hard with the heel of your palm. Discard the skin.

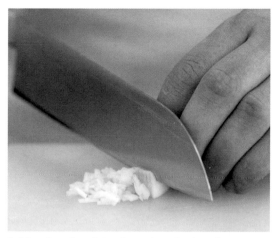

2 Slice the clove into slivers lengthwise, then cut across to make tiny chunks. Gather the pieces into a pile and chop again for finer pieces.

Chop herbs

Use a large, sharp knife to chop fresh herbs just before you use them to release their flavor and aroma.

1 Strip the leaves from their stems and gather them together in a tight pile. With basil leaves (shown), layer the leaves and roll them gently.

2 Chop through the pile of herbs using a rocking motion with the knife. Gather again and repeat to achieve the desired size.

Zucchini, herb, and lemon tagine

A flavorful vegetarian version of the famous Moroccan speciality.

INGREDIENTS

2 tbsp olive oil
2 red onions, finely chopped
salt and freshly ground black pepper
4 garlic cloves, finely chopped
pinch of fennel seeds
pinch of ground cinnamon
2–3 tsp harissa (or to taste)
4 preserved lemons, halved,
   pith removed, and halved again
one 28oz (800g) can whole
   tomatoes, chopped

1 head broccoli, broken into florets
6 zucchini, sliced
juice of 1 lemon
handful of dill, finely chopped
14oz (400g) couscous
handful of parsley, finely chopped
harissa and lemon wedges, to serve

METHOD

1 Heat half the oil in a large heavy-based pan, add the onions, and cook over low heat for 5 minutes, or until soft. Season. Stir in the garlic, fennel seeds, cinnamon, harissa, and lemons.

2 Add the tomatoes and stir well, crushing them with the back of a wooden spoon. Bring to a boil, then reduce to a simmer and cook over low heat for 30–40 minutes, or until the fennel is soft. If the sauce starts to dry out, add a little hot water.

3 Meanwhile, cook the broccoli in a pan of boiling salted water for 3–5 minutes or until tender, then drain and refresh in cold water. Drain again and set aside. Heat the rest of the oil in the frying pan, add the zucchini, and season with salt and pepper. Cook over low heat, stirring frequently, for 5 minutes, or until the zucchini start to color a little. Add a squeeze of lemon and stir in the dill.

4 Meanwhile, put the couscous in a large bowl and pour in just enough boiling water to cover it. Set aside for 10 minutes, then fluff with a fork and season with salt and pepper. Add the broccoli and zucchini to the sauce and stir in the parsley. Serve with the couscous, lemon wedges, and harissa.

8 servings

prep 25 mins
• cook 40 mins

healthy option

Provençal lamb

This French-style big-pot dish requires little effort and will keep a hungry horde happy.

INGREDIENTS

4 tbsp olive oil
4 onions, cut into eighths
2½lb (1.1kg) leg of lamb, cut into
   bite-size chunks
2 tsp paprika
6 garlic cloves, chopped
6 tbsp black olives
2 tbsp capers
4 tsp dried oregano
2 tsp dried thyme
6 tbsp dry (fino) sherry
salt and freshly ground black pepper
two 28oz (1.6kg) cans diced tomatoes

METHOD

1 Preheat the oven to 300°F (150°C). Heat the oil in the casserole over medium heat, add the onions, and cook for 5 minutes or until starting to soften. Add the lamb and paprika and cook, turning frequently, for 8–10 minutes or until the lamb is no longer pink.

2 Add the garlic, olives, capers, oregano, thyme, and sherry and cook for 3 minutes. Season with salt and pepper, add the tomatoes, stir well, and bring to a boil. Cover the pan with a well-fitting lid and transfer to the oven for 2½ hours.

GOOD WITH Herbed mashed potatoes and olive oil.

8 servings

**prep 25 mins
• cook 2 hrs
30 mins**

**large flame-proof
casserole**

**freeze for up to
3 months**

Spanish-style chicken with pine nuts

Slow-cooked in wine and tomatoes, this chicken is deliciously tender.

INGREDIENTS
2 tbsp olive oil
8 chicken thighs
1 onion, finely chopped
salt and freshly ground black pepper
3 garlic cloves, finely chopped
6 ripe tomatoes, peeled and chopped
$\frac{1}{2}$ cup dry red wine
4 cups hot chicken stock
handful of pine nuts, toasted
handful of golden raisins (optional)

METHOD
1 In a large cast-iron or other flame-proof casserole, heat 1 tbsp of the oil over medium-high heat. Add the chicken and cook for about 5 minutes on each side until golden all over. Remove from the pan, and set aside.

2 Reduce the heat to medium. Add the remaining oil, the onion, and a pinch of salt to the same pan, and cook for about 5 minutes until soft.

3 Stir in the garlic and fresh tomatoes, and season with pepper. Cook for a few minutes until the tomatoes start to break down. Add the red wine, increase the heat slightly, and let bubble for a few minutes.

4 Stir in the hot stock and bring to a boil. Reduce the heat to low and return the chicken to the pan along with the pine nuts and raisins (if using). Gently simmer for 30–40 minutes, adding a little hot water if the mixture becomes dry. Serve hot.

GOOD WITH Rice or boiled new potatoes.

4 servings

**prep 10 mins
• cook 1 hr**

**large flame-proof
casserole**

Pork and bean stew

Otherwise known as *Feijoada*, this is the national dish of Brazil and is made with a variety of porks.

INGREDIENTS

1 cup dried black-eyed beans
2 pigs' feet
9oz (250g) smoked pork spareribs, smoked pork chops, or cubed ham
6oz (175g) slab bacon, in one piece
1 cup canned chopped tomatoes
1 tbsp tomato paste
1 bay leaf
salt and freshly ground black pepper
2 tbsp vegetable oil

1lb (450g) boneless center-cut pork loin, cut into thick slices
1 onion, finely chopped
2 garlic cloves, finely chopped
6oz (175g) chorizo, diced
1 green chile, seeded and minced (optional)
1 orange, cut into wedges, to garnish
3 spring onions, white and green parts, chopped, to garnish

METHOD

1 Rinse and drain the beans. Place in a bowl and add enough cold water to cover by 1in (2.5cm). Let stand at room temperature for 8–12 hours.

2 Drain the beans and place in a soup pot. Cover with fresh water and bring to the boil over high heat. Boil for 10 minutes, skimming off any foam. Lower the heat and cover. Simmer for 1 hour.

3 Meanwhile, place the pigs' feet, ribs, and bacon in a large saucepan with the tomatoes, tomato paste, and bay leaf. Add enough cold water to cover and bring to a boil over high heat. Reduce the heat to low and cover the pot. Simmer for 50 minutes. Season with salt and pepper.

4 Drain the beans in a colander, reserving the cooking liquid. Return the beans to the pot and add the meats with their cooking liquid. Add enough of the reserved bean liquid to barely cover. Return to a boil. Reduce the heat to medium-low, cover, and simmer for 20 minutes.

5 Heat 1 tbsp of the oil in a large frying pan over medium-high heat. In batches, add the pork tenderloin and brown on both sides. Add the pork tenderloin to the simmering bean mixture and cook for 10 minutes more, or until the meats are tender and the beans are very soft. Wipe out the frying pan. Heat the remaining oil, add the onion and garlic and cook, stirring frequently, about 4 minutes, until soft and translucent. Add the chorizo and chile, if using, and cook for 2 minutes more, stirring often. Add 3 tbsp of the cooked beans and mash well with the back of a spoon. Stir the mashed beans and sausage into the pot of beans, and cook for 10 minutes.

6 To serve, remove the larger pieces of meat and cut them up. Spread the beans in a wide serving bowl, and top with the meats. Garnish with the orange wedges and scallions and serve hot.

GOOD WITH Cooked white rice, steamed or fried shredded kale, and a tomato salsa.

PREPARE AHEAD The stew can be made a day in advance and reheated.

8 servings

prep 1hr 15 mins, plus soaking
• cook 1hr 25 mins

soak the beans overnight

Hungarian goulash

This warming winter stew makes a great main course if you are entertaining, as all the hard work can be done in advance.

INGREDIENTS

4 tbsp vegetable oil
2lb (900g) beef chuck, cut into 1in (2.5cm) cubes
2 large onions, thinly sliced
2 red bell peppers, seeded and chopped
2 garlic cloves, finely chopped
1 tbsp paprika, plus more to garnish
one 14.5oz (411g) can chopped tomatoes, drained
2 tbsp tomato paste
1 tbsp all-purpose flour
1¼ cups beef stock
1 tsp chopped thyme
salt and freshly ground black pepper
⅔ cup sour cream

METHOD

1 Preheat the oven to 325°F (160°C). Heat 2 tbsp of the oil in a large casserole over medium-high heat. Add the beef in batches, and cook for about 5 minutes, turning occasionally, until browned.

2 Add the remaining oil to the casserole and reduce the heat to medium. Add the onions, peppers, and garlic, and cook, scraping up the bits in the casserole, about 5 minutes, until the onions are transparent. Add the paprika and stir for 1 minute.

3 Stir in the tomatoes and tomato paste. Dissolve the flour in ¼ cup of the stock, then stir into the casserole with the remaining stock and thyme, and season to taste. Bring to a boil, stirring often.

4 Cover tightly. Bake for 2 hours, or until the beef is tender.

5 To serve, spoon the goulash into individual bowls. Top each with a generous dollop of sour cream and sprinkle with a little paprika.

GOOD WITH Buttered tagliatelle.

4 servings

prep 25 mins
• cook 2 hrs
30 mins

healthy option

freeze, without
the sour cream,
for up to 3 months

Chicken with cider and cream

This casserole is simple to make but a treat to eat.

INGREDIENTS
about 1 tbsp olive oil
2 onions, cut into 8 wedges
2 garlic cloves, finely chopped
8 chicken thighs
1¼ cups hard cider, apple cider,
   or unsweetened apple juice
1¼ cups heavy whipping cream
a few sprigs of rosemary
salt and freshly ground black pepper

METHOD

1 Preheat the oven to 400°F (200°C). Heat 1 tbsp olive oil in a large cast-iron or other flame-proof casserole over medium-low heat. Add the onion and a pinch of salt, and cook for 5 minutes until soft. Now add the garlic, and cook for 10 seconds.

2 Push the onions to one side of the casserole, and increase the heat to medium-high. Add a little more oil if needed, and add the chicken thighs, skin-side down. Brown for about 10 minutes, turning once, until golden.

3 Increase the heat slightly and pour in the cider. Let bubble for a few minutes, then reduce the heat to a simmer, and add the cream. Add the rosemary sprigs, and season well with salt and pepper.

4 Cover, and transfer to the oven to cook for about 40 minutes. If it is becoming too dry, add a little hot water or stock. Serve hot.

GOOD WITH Mashed potatoes and fresh crusty bread, to mop up the juices.

4 servings

**prep 10 mins
• cook 1 hr**

**large flame-proof
casserole**

Aduki bean stew

Sweet, nutty aduki beans give this stew its body and texture.

INGREDIENTS
1 tbsp olive oil
1 onion, finely chopped
salt and freshly ground black pepper
2 garlic cloves, finely chopped
$\frac{1}{2}$–1 tsp cayenne pepper (depending on taste)
one 15oz (425g) can aduki beans, drained and rinsed
one 14oz (400g) can diced tomatoes, with juices
2 cups hot vegetable stock
about 12 black olives, such as Kalamata, pitted

METHOD
1 Heat the olive oil in a saucepan over low heat. Add the onion and a pinch of salt, and cook gently for 5 minutes until soft. Stir in the garlic and cayenne.

2 Add the beans and tomatoes, including any juices, then pour in the stock. Bring to a boil, then reduce the heat to low.

3 Simmer for 15–20 minutes, stirring in the olives during the last 5 minutes of cooking. If the stew dries out, add a little hot water.

GOOD WITH A crisp salad, new potatoes, or rice.

4 servings

prep 10 mins
• cook 30 mins

healthy option

freeze for up to
3 months

Braised oxtail with wine and herbs

Oxtail is high in gelatin, which gives extraordinary texture to the sauce in this robust dish.

INGREDIENTS

6½lb (3kg) oxtail, cut into 1½in (3.5cm) lengths
½ cup all-purpose flour
4 tbsp olive oil
1 tbsp honey
2 tbsp chopped thyme
2 tbsp chopped rosemary
salt and freshly ground black pepper
2 onions, chopped
2 carrots, cut into large chunks
1 fennel, diced
2 garlic cloves, sliced
2 fresh hot red chiles, chopped
one 750ml bottle hearty red wine
chopped parsley, to garnish

METHOD

1 Preheat the oven to 300°F (150°C). Toss the oxtail in flour to coat lightly. Heat 2 tbsp of the oil in a large frying pan over medium-high heat. In batches, add the oxtail and cook, turning occasionally, about 5 minutes, until browned. Transfer to a large casserole.

2 Drizzle the honey over the oxtail. Sprinkle with the thyme and rosemary, and season with salt and pepper.

3 Heat the remaining oil in the frying pan. Add the vegetables, garlic, and chiles and cook for 6 minutes, until softened. Stir into casserole and add the wine. Cover and bake for 2–3 hours, until the oxtail is very tender. Skim the fat from the surface of the sauce. Garnish with chopped parsley and serve hot.

GOOD WITH Creamy mashed potatoes.

PREPARE AHEAD The stew can be cooled, covered, and refrigerated for up to 2 days; it gets better as it rests.

6 servings

prep 20 mins
• cook 2–3 hrs

freeze for up to
3 months

Quick fish pie

Homely and filling, this pie is a British classic. It could also be made with any leftover seafood and mashed potatoes.

INGREDIENTS

2lb (900g) russet or other baking potatoes, peeled and quartered

1 tbsp butter, plus extra for topping, if desired

1½lb (675g) skinless boneless white fish, such as haddock, hake, sustainable cod, or pollack, cut into chunks

⅔ cup whole milk

1 cup frozen peas

4 hard-boiled eggs, peeled and chopped (optional)

salt and freshly ground black pepper

For the sauce

2 tbsp (30g) butter

3 tbsp (25g) all-purpose flour

1¼ cups whole milk, or as needed

1 tbsp Dijon mustard

salt and freshly ground black pepper

METHOD

1 Preheat the oven to 400°F (200°C), or the broiler to high. Peel and quarter the potatoes, and boil or steam in a pan of salted water for about 15 minutes, or until soft. Drain well, and mash. Add the butter, and mash again. Set aside and keep warm.

2 Put the fish in a shallow frying pan. Season well with salt and pepper. Pour in just enough of the milk to cover, and poach over medium heat for 3–4 minutes. Remove the fish with a slotted spoon, and transfer to a baking dish.

3 To make the sauce, melt the butter in a saucepan over medium heat. Remove from the heat, and stir in the flour with a wooden spoon until smooth. Return the pan to the heat, and gradually add the milk, stirring constantly. Keep cooking and stirring for 5–6 minutes until the sauce has thickened. Add more milk if needed. Stir in the mustard and season with salt and pepper. Gently stir in the peas and eggs.

4 Spoon the sauce over the fish, and stir gently. Top with the reserved mashed potatoes, swirling the surface with a spoon to form peaks. Dot with extra butter if desired, then bake or cook under a hot broiler for about 10 minutes, or until the top is crisp and golden and the mixture is heated through.

PREPARE AHEAD The potatoes and fish could be cooked the day before and kept chilled until needed. Bring the mashed potatoes back to room temperature before using it to top the pie.

4 servings

prep 15 mins
• cook 20 mins

freeze for up to
3 months

Chicken with pancetta, peas, and mint

Sweet peas, white wine, and fragrant mint give this dish a taste of summer.

INGREDIENTS
2 tbsp olive oil
4 large or 8 small chicken pieces such thighs and breasts,
 about 1½lb (675g) total, skin on
2 onions, finely chopped
7oz (200g) pancetta, cubed
2 garlic cloves, finely chopped
1 cup dry white wine
2½ cups chicken stock
salt and freshly ground black pepper
8–10oz (225–300g) frozen peas
handful of parsley, finely chopped
handful of mint leaves, finely chopped

METHOD
1 Preheat the oven to 300°F (150°C). Heat 1 tbsp of the oil in a large flame-proof casserole over medium heat. Add the chicken pieces, and cook for about 8 minutes, turning, until golden. Remove the chicken pieces from the pan, and set aside.

2 Reduce the heat to low, and add the remaining oil and onions to the casserole. Cook gently for 5 minutes until soft, then add the pancetta. Increase the heat a little, and cook for another 5 minutes until the pancetta is browned. Stir in the garlic, then pour in the wine. Increase the heat to high, and let bubble for few minutes until the alcohol has evaporated.

3 Add the stock, and bring to a boil once again. Season with salt and pepper, and stir in the peas, parsley, and mint. Return the chicken pieces to the casserole, cover, and transfer to the oven to cook for 1½ hours. Check the level of liquid occasionally while cooking—it needs to be fairly dry, but if it does require more liquid to prevent sticking, just add a little hot water. Serve hot.

GOOD WITH Fresh crusty bread or sautéed potatoes.

4 servings

**prep 15 mins
• cook 1 hr
45 mins**

**large flame-proof
casserole**

Chickpea and vegetable stew

This dish tastes better the next day as the flavors mature—simply reheat any leftovers.

INGREDIENTS

1 tbsp olive oil
1 onion, finely chopped
2 garlic cloves, finely chopped
3 celery ribs, finely chopped
3 carrots, finely chopped
$\frac{1}{2}$ cup dry white wine
one 14oz (400g) can diced tomatoes
one 15$\frac{1}{2}$oz (439g) can chickpeas (garbanzo beans),
   drained and rinsed
$\frac{2}{3}$ cup hot vegetable stock
handful of fresh green beans, sliced on the diagonal
salt and freshly ground black pepper

METHOD

1 Heat the oil in a large saucepan over low heat. Add the onion and a pinch of salt, and cook for about 5 minutes until soft. Stir in the garlic, celery, and carrots, and cook 5 minutes longer.

2 Increase the heat, add the wine, and let bubble until the alcohol has cooked away. Add the tomatoes, bring to a boil, and pour in the stock. Add the chickpeas, reduce the heat slightly, and simmer gently for 15 minutes.

3 Add the green beans, and cook for 5–10 minutes, until tender. Season well with salt and pepper. Serve hot.

GOOD WITH Crusty bread.

4 servings

prep 15 mins
• cook 35 mins

healthy option

freeze for up
to 3 months

Beef and leek couscous

Filling enough to be served as a main course, this is a convenient dish for feeding a hungry crowd.

INGREDIENTS
$\frac{1}{2}$ cup olive oil
6 leeks, cleaned and finely sliced
$1\frac{1}{2}$ lb (675g) ground beef
2 red chiles, seeded and finely chopped
2 tsp paprika
6 garlic cloves, sliced
$\frac{2}{3}$ cup dry white wine
2 cups hot beef stock
handful of parsley, finely chopped
1lb (450g) couscous

METHOD
1 Preheat the oven to 300°F (150°C). Heat the oil in a large flame-proof casserole, add the leeks, and cook over medium heat for 5 minutes. Add the ground beef and cook, stirring occasionally, for 10 minutes or until no longer pink.

2 Stir in the chiles, paprika, and garlic and cook for 2 minutes. Pour in the wine and cook for 3 minutes, then add the stock and parsley and combine well. Stir in the couscous, then cover with a lid and cook in the oven for 15 minutes. Stir and serve.

serves 6–8

prep 25 mins
• cook 15 mins

large flameproof
casserole

Smoked fish and anchovy gratin

A creamy and flavorful fish dish with a crisp, golden topping.

INGREDIENTS

9oz (250g) smoked fish, such as mackerel and salmon,
    thinly sliced or broken into small chunks
8–12 anchovies in oil, drained
4 all-purpose waxy potatoes, peeled, boiled, and sliced
1–2 tbsp butter, melted, boiled, and sliced
knob of butter, melted

For the sauce

1 tbsp butter
1 onion, finely chopped
1 garlic clove, finely chopped
1 tbsp all-purpose flour
1¼ cups whole milk
handful of parsley, finely chopped
salt and freshly ground black pepper

METHOD

1 Preheat the oven to 400°F (200°C).

2 To make the sauce, melt the butter in a saucepan over low heat. Add the onion, and cook gently for about 5 minutes until soft, then add the garlic and cook for a few seconds longer. Remove from the heat and stir in the flour with a wooden spoon, then beat in a little of the milk until smooth.

3 Return the pan to the heat, and slowly add the rest of the milk, whisking until thickened. Season with salt and pepper, and stir in the parsley.

4 Layer the fish and anchovies in an oven-proof dish, then cover with the sauce. Top with an even layer of potatoes, brush with melted butter, and bake in the oven for 15–20 minutes or until the potatoes are golden and crispy and the fish is heated through.

GOOD WITH A crisp green salad.

4 servings

prep 10 mins
• cook 30 mins

healthy option

Spicy lamb with baby potatoes

Warm, North African flavors enliven this dish.

INGREDIENTS
1½lb (675g) lean lamb,
    cut into ¾in (2cm) cubes
3 tsp paprika
1 tsp cayenne pepper
finely grated zest of 2 lemons
10 tbsp olive oil
3 onions, finely diced
2½lb (1.1kg) small creamer potatoes
large handful parsley, finely chopped
6 garlic cloves, finely chopped
2 tbsp finely chopped thyme
1 tbsp chopped rosemary leaves
6 preserved lemons, quartered
    and pith removed
salt and freshly ground black pepper

METHOD
1 Preheat the oven to 300°F (150°C). Put the lamb, paprika, cayenne, and lemon zest in a mixing bowl, combine well, then set aside. Heat 4 tbsp of the oil in a large flame-proof casserole, add the onions, and cook over medium heat for 3 minutes. Add the lamb and cook, stirring frequently, for 5 minutes or until no longer pink.

2 Add the potatoes and cook for 2 minutes, then add the parsley, garlic, thyme, rosemary, preserved lemons, and the rest of the olive oil. Combine and toss together, season with salt and pepper, and cover with a lid. Place the pan in the oven and cook, stirring frequently, for 1½ hours. Serve warm.

GOOD WITH Herbed couscous or rice.

6–8 servings

**prep 25 mins
• cook 1 hr
30 mins**

**large flame-proof
casserole**

Beef and tomato lasagna

A dollop of pesto perks up the flavors in this family favorite.

INGREDIENTS

6 tbsp olive oil

3 large onions, finely diced

1½lb (675g) lean ground beef

8 garlic cloves, chopped

3 tbsp tomato paste or purée

three 14oz (400g) cans diced tomatoes

2 tsp dried oregano

4 bay leaves

salt and freshly ground black pepper

3 tsp pesto

3 tbsp butter

3 heaping tbsp all-purpose flour

3½ cups milk

10oz (300g) mozzarella, grated

1lb (450g) oven-ready lasagna

METHOD

1 Heat the oil in a large heavy-based saucepan over medium heat, add the onions, and cook, stirring occasionally, for 5 minutes or until starting to soften. Add the ground beef and cook, stirring constantly, for 5 minutes, or until no longer pink. Add the garlic, cook for 1 minute, then stir in the tomato paste. Add the tomatoes, oregano, and bay leaves, bring to a boil, then reduce the heat and simmer for 20 minutes. Season with salt and pepper, remove from heat, then stir in the pesto and set aside.

2 Melt the butter in a saucepan over low heat, add the flour, and stir well. Add a little of the milk, mix well, then add ⅔ cup more milk, stirring vigorously until smooth. Add the rest of the milk, combine well, then bring to a boil, stirring constantly. Reduce the heat and simmer for 2 minutes to ensure the flour is cooked. Remove from heat, stir in the mozzarella, then season with salt and pepper.

3 Preheat the oven to 350°F (180°C). Pour ½in (1cm) of the beef sauce in the bottom of a large baking pan (or 2 medium-sized ones). Cover with a layer of lasagna noodles, then add ½in (1cm) more beef sauce, followed by a small amount of the cheese sauce and another layer of lasagna. Repeat until all the meat sauce has been used up. Make sure you have enough cheese sauce for an even ¼in (5mm) layer on the top.

4 Bake in the oven for 35–40 minutes, or until browned on top and piping hot inside.

GOOD WITH A green salad drizzled with olive oil and balsamic vinegar.

PREPARE AHEAD This recipe serves 8, so is perfect if you want to divide it and freeze some. Assemble the lasagna in an freezer-proof baking pan, then let it cool completely before double-wrapping in plastic wrap and freezing. To serve, remove the plastic wrap and put it straight in an oven preheated to 350°F (180°C) for 35–40 minutes, or until piping hot.

8 servings

prep 30 mins
• cook 35–40 mins

freeze for up to
3 months

Sausage and mustard casserole

This is pure winter bliss. Serve it with creamy mashed potatoes and it will remain a favorite.

INGREDIENTS
1 tbsp olive oil
12 Italian sweet pork sausages
1 large onion, thinly sliced
8oz (225g) cremini mushrooms
1¼ cups chicken stock
1 Granny Smith apple, peeled, cored, and cut into chunks
1 tbsp chopped sage
1 bay leaf
²/₃ cup heavy cream
salt and freshly ground black pepper
2 tsp Dijon mustard
1 tsp whole grain mustard
1 tsp dry mustard

METHOD
1 Heat the oil in a large flame-proof casserole over medium heat. Add the sausages, cook until golden, and remove.

2 Add the onion and cook until softened. Add the mushrooms and cook for 5 minutes, then stir in the stock, apple, sage, and bay leaf.

3 Bring to a boil, then return the sausages. Reduce the heat, cover, and cook gently for 20 minutes, stirring often. The apple pieces should break down and thicken the sauce slightly. If they are still holding their shape, mash them with the back of a wooden spoon and stir in.

4 Mix the cream and mustards together in a bowl and season with salt and pepper. Pour into the casserole, increase the heat, and boil gently for 5 minutes, or until the sauce has thickened slightly.

GOOD WITH Cabbage and creamy mashed potatoes.

6 servings

**prep 15 mins
• cook 45 mins**

large flame-proof casserole

Spiced bean and herb hash

This medley of chopped potatoes and chili beans makes a hearty breakfast or brunch.

INGREDIENTS

1 tsp olive oil, plus extra as needed
1 tbsp butter
1 red onion, coarsely chopped
handful of thyme sprigs, leaves picked
1lb (450g) russet (baking) potatoes,
    peeled and cubed
one 14oz (400g) can chili beans
$^2/_3$ cup hot vegetable stock
handful of parsley, finely chopped
salt and freshly ground black pepper

METHOD

1 Heat the oil and butter in a nonstick frying pan over low heat. Add the onion, a pinch of salt, and the thyme leaves, and cook for about 5 minutes until the onion is soft.

2 Add the potatoes and cook until lightly browned at the edges—you may need to add more olive oil to accomplish this.

3 When the potatoes are nearly tender—about 15 minutes—stir in the chili beans. Pour in the hot stock and simmer for 10 minutes. Stir in the parsley and season well with salt and pepper. Serve hot.

4 servings

prep 10 mins
• cook 30 mins

healthy option

freeze for up to
3 months

Baby zucchini with fish and couscous

Wholesome and hearty, this dish nevertheless has fresh, zesty flavors that you can enjoy in summer.

INGREDIENTS

$\frac{1}{2}$ cup olive oil

1lb 5oz (600g) baby zucchini, halved lengthwise

juice and finely grated zest of 2 limes

3 tbsp tomato paste

1 tsp five-spice powder

1 tsp cayenne pepper

2 tsp paprika

1 tsp freshly ground black pepper

large handful of parsley, finely chopped

4 garlic cloves, finely chopped

1$\frac{1}{4}$lb (550g) white fish, such as haddock,
   cut into bite-size pieces

2 cups hot vegetable stock

1lb (450g) couscous

METHOD

1 Preheat the oven to 300°F (150°C). Put 2 tbsp of the oil in a bowl, add the zucchini, and mix until evenly coated. Cook in a hot ridged cast-iron grill pan or frying pan for 2 minutes on each side, then set aside. You may need to do this in batches.

2 Add the rest of the oil to the bowl, and mix with the lime juice and zest, tomato paste, five-spice powder, cayenne, paprika, black pepper, parsley, and garlic. Then add the fish, stock, couscous, and zucchini and combine carefully.

3 Transfer to a baking pan and cover with foil. Cook in the oven for 20 minutes, then stir and serve.

6–8 servings

prep 20 mins
• cook 25 mins

healthy option

ridged cast-iron
grill pan

Spicy garlic green vegetable medley

A quick, Asian-inspired vegetarian stir-fry.

INGREDIENTS
handful of hazelnuts
1 tbsp sesame oil or vegetable oil
3 garlic cloves, thinly sliced
2 fresh green jalapeño chile peppers,
    seeded and finely chopped
1 tbsp soy sauce
1 tbsp Chinese rice wine
1–2 heads bok choy, quartered lengthwise
handful of fresh spinach leaves or Swiss chard
2 handfuls of sugar snap peas or snow peas, sliced into thin strips
salt and freshly ground black pepper

METHOD
1 Spread the hazelnuts on a baking sheet. Toast under a hot broiler until golden brown, shaking the pan frequently. Put the hazelnuts in a clean dish towel and rub off the skins. Chop coarsely and set aside.

2 Heat the oil in a wok over medium-high heat, and swirl it around to coat the pan. Add the garlic and chiles and cook for 10 seconds, then add the soy sauce and Chinese rice wine, and cook for a few seconds more.

3 Add the bok choy and spinach, and stir-fry for 1 minute. Add the sugar snap peas, and stir-fry for 1 more minute. Toss well, then season with salt and pepper. Serve immediately with the hazelnuts scattered over the top.

GOOD WITH Hot, fluffy rice.

servings 4

prep 15 mins
• cook 15 mins

healthy option

wok

Pork and spring greens

Get the most from your roast—this is a perfect dish for using up leftovers.

INGREDIENTS

1 tbsp olive oil
12oz (350g) cooked pork,
   coarsely shredded
4 garlic cloves, thinly sliced
2 heads of collard greens or
   other leafy greens, shredded
2 tsp onion seeds (optional)
salt and freshly ground black pepper

METHOD

1 Heat the oil in a wok over medium-high heat. When the oil is hot, add the pork. Cook for about 5 minutes, stirring and tossing it in the pan.

2 Add the garlic and the greens, and continue to stir-fry over medium-high heat for 1 minute, or until the greens have just wilted. Stir in the onion seeds, then season well with salt and pepper. Serve immediately.

GOOD WITH Roast new potatoes.

4 servings

prep 10 mins
• cook 10 mins

healthy option

wok

Crispy rice noodles with beef

This tasty dish is a combination of crunchy textures and Asian flavors.

INGREDIENTS

vegetable oil, as needed

5oz (140g) dried rice vermicelli

3 tbsp soy sauce

2 tbsp oyster sauce

1 tbsp light brown sugar

12oz (350g) sirloin steak or filet mignon,
    thinly sliced

2 garlic cloves, thinly sliced

1 tsp peeled and shredded fresh ginger

12 thin asparagus spears,
    cut into 1in (2.5cm) lengths

6 scallions, white and green parts,
    cut into 1in (2.5cm) lengths

1/4 cup chopped cashews

Asian sesame oil, for serving

METHOD

1 Heat 2in (5cm) oil in a deep-fat fryer or large saucepan over high heat. Break the vermicelli into 7 or 8 portions. In batches, add to the hot oil and cook for a few seconds until they turn white and become crisp. Transfer to paper towels. Keep warm.

2 Mix the soy sauce, oyster sauce, sugar, and 1 tbsp water. Heat 2 tbsp oil in a wok over high heat, stir-fry the beef for 2 minutes, until browned. Transfer to a plate.

3 Add 1 tbsp oil, and stir-fry the garlic and ginger for 30 seconds. Add the asparagus and scallions, stir-fry for 2 minutes, then add the sauce and beef to the pan. Stir-fry until the sauce is thick and boiling. Divide the rice vermicelli among 4 plates. Pile the stir-fry on top, top with cashews, drizzle with sesame oil, and serve immediately.

4 servings

prep 20 mins
• cook 15 mins

deep-fat fryer or
large saucepan
• wok

Hokkien noodles with pork

Chinese barbecued pork (also called char-sui), pork loin cooked with a shiny scarlet glaze, and fresh Hokkien-style noodles can be purchased at Asian grocers.

INGREDIENTS

½ cup dried cloud ear (tree fungus) mushrooms

2 tbsp oyster sauce

2 tbsp soy sauce

1 tsp honey

2 tbsp vegetable oil

2 garlic cloves, minced

2 tsp peeled and finely grated
   fresh ginger

1 red bell pepper, seeded and
   thinly sliced

1 cup snow peas, each cut in
   half lengthwise

1lb (450g) thick fresh Hokkein-style egg noodles

12oz (350g) char-sui pork, thinly sliced

METHOD

1 Put the mushrooms in a heat-proof bowl, cover with boiling water, and set aside for 30 minutes to soak. Drain and cut the mushrooms into thin strips.

2 Bring a large pot of water to a boil over high heat. Mix the oyster sauce, soy sauce, and honey together in a small bowl.

3 Heat the oil in a wok or frying pan over high heat. Add the garlic and ginger and stir-fry for 15 seconds. Add the red pepper, stir-fry for 3 minutes, then add the snow peas, and stir-fry for 1 minute, until they turn bright green.

4 Meanwhile, add the noodles to the boiling water and cook for 1 minute. Add the pork to the wok, pour in the oyster sauce mixture and toss over the heat for 1 minute, until everything is heated. Drain the noodles, mix with the stir-fried pork and vegetables, and serve hot.

4–6 servings

**prep 20 mins,
plus soaking
• cook 10 mins**

Parsi eggs

This Indian dish has its origins in ancient Persia.

INGREDIENTS

4 tbsp butter
4 scallions, thinly sliced
1 tsp peeled, grated fresh ginger
1 large fresh hot red or green chile,
  seeded and minced
2 tsp curry powder
4 tomatoes, seeded and chopped
8 large eggs
2 tbsp whole milk
salt and freshly ground black pepper
2 tbsp chopped cilantro

METHOD

1 Melt 2 tbsp butter in a large nonstick frying pan over low heat. Add the scallions, ginger, and chile and cook, stirring occasionally, for 2 minutes.

2 Stir in the curry powder. Add the tomatoes and cook for 1 minute. Transfer to a plate.

3 Add the remaining 2 tbsp butter to the pan and melt. Whisk the eggs and milk together, and season with salt and pepper. Pour into the pan and stir until scrambled and almost set. Add the vegetables, stir well, and cook until just set. Sprinkle with cilantro and serve at once.

GOOD WITH Salad leaves, light toasted naan bread, or chapatis.

4 servings

prep 10 mins
• cook 15 mins

Chicken with noodles and basil

Herbs from the basil family grow widely in South-East Asia and lend an authentic flavor to noodles.

INGREDIENTS

1 tbsp sesame oil
2 large skinless boneless chicken breast halves, sliced
1 tbsp soy sauce
1 tbsp honey
10oz (300g) thick or medium ready-to-use udon noodles
handful of basil leaves, torn

METHOD

1 Heat the oil in a large wok or frying pan over medium-high heat. When hot, swirl it around the pan, and add the chicken. Stir-fry quickly for a few minutes until beginning to turn golden. Remove from the pan, and set aside to keep warm.

2 Add the soy sauce and honey to the pan, and let bubble for a minute or so. Return the chicken to the pan along with the noodles, and stir so that everything is well coated.

3 When ready to serve, stir in the basil. Serve immediately.

4 servings

prep 5 mins
• cook 15 mins

healthy option

Chickpeas with spinach

Chickpeas are widely used in Spain as a basis for a variety of beautifully seasoned dishes such as this one.

INGREDIENTS

3 tbsp olive oil
1 thick slice of crusty white bread,
   torn into small pieces
1lb 10oz (750g) leaf spinach
one 8.5oz (240g) can chickpeas,
   drained and rinsed
2 garlic cloves, finely chopped
1 tsp sweet paprika
1 tsp ground cumin
salt and freshly ground black pepper
1 tbsp sherry vinegar

METHOD

1 Heat 2 tbsp of oil in a frying pan. Add the torn bread and fry, stirring occasionally, until crisp. Transfer to paper towels to drain.

2 Remove any thick stems from the spinach. Wash the spinach well and shake off any excess water. Put the spinach in a large saucepan and cook over low heat, stirring often until it has wilted. Drain in a colander and cool. A handful at a time, squeeze out as much liquid as possible. Transfer to a chopping board and chop coarsely.

3 Add the remaining oil in the frying pan over medium-high heat. Add the garlic and cook for 1 minute. Then add the spinach and cook, stirring often, about 3 minutes, until warmed through. Add the chickpeas, paprika, and cumin. Season with salt and pepper. Crumble in the fried bread.

4 Add the vinegar and 2 tbsp water, and cook, stirring often, about 5 minutes, until the chickpeas are hot. Serve immediately.

4 servings

prep 15 mins
• cook 10 mins

Chicken stir-fried with scallions, basil, and lemon grass

Cornstarch gives the chicken a light, crispy coating to complement the fresh flavors of this healthy stir-fry.

INGREDIENTS

2–3 skinless boneless chicken breast halves,
    about 7oz (200g) each, sliced into strips
1 tbsp cornstarch
2 tbsp Asian sesame oil
bunch of scallions, sliced on the diagonal
3 garlic cloves, sliced
1 stalk fresh lemon grass, tough outer leaves removed, chopped
2 fresh red mild chile peppers, seeded and sliced
1 tbsp Chinese rice wine
handful of basil leaves
salt and freshly ground black pepper

METHOD

1 Season the chicken with salt and pepper. Put the cornstarch in a bowl, and toss the chicken strips in it until very well coated.

2 Heat 1 tbsp of the oil in a wok over high heat. Swirl around the pan, then add the chicken and stir-fry quickly, moving the chicken around the pan for 3–5 minutes until golden and cooked through. Remove with a slotted spoon and set aside to keep warm.

3 Carefully wipe out the wok with paper towels, reduce the heat to medium-high, and add the remaining oil. When hot, add the scallions, garlic, lemon grass, and chiles. Stir-fry for a couple of minutes, then increase the heat to high once again, and add the rice wine. Let bubble for a few minutes.

4 Return the chicken to the pan to just heat through, stir in the basil, and serve at once.

GOOD WITH Hot, fluffy rice.

4 servings

**prep 10 mins
• cook 15 mins**

healthy option

wok

Chicken livers with shallots and arugula

Livers have a rich taste and make a satisfying supper. Avoid overcooking them though, as this will make them tough.

INGREDIENTS
$\frac{1}{2}$ cup hazelnuts
1 tbsp olive oil
9 small shallots, peeled but left whole
1–2 tbsp demerara (raw) sugar
1 tbsp butter
250g (9oz) chicken livers, tossed
  in a little seasoned flour
2 handfuls of arugula leaves
generous drizzle of balsamic vinegar
salt

METHOD
1 Spread hazelnuts on a baking sheet. Place under a hot broiler and shake the pan frequently to turn them, until they are golden brown. Enclose the hazelnuts in a clean dish towel. Rub to loosen and remove the skins. Chop coarsely, and set aside.

2 Heat the oil in a large frying pan over medium heat. Add the shallots, and cook for 5 minutes until they start to color slightly, then sprinkle with some salt and the sugar. Move the shallots around in the pan, and cook for another 15 minutes or until they soften and begin to caramelize.

3 In a separate frying pan, heat the butter over medium-high heat. When melted and foaming, add the chicken livers. Cook for 3–5 minutes, turning once, until browned on the outside and just cooked through.

4 Cut the cooked shallots in half, and arrange with the livers on a bed of arugula leaves. Top with the toasted hazelnuts, and drizzle with the balsamic vinegar. Serve at once.

GOOD WITH Thick slices of whole-wheat toast.

4 servings

prep 15 mins
• cook 20 mins

Ground beef and chickpeas cooked with orange and cinnamon

Moroccan-inspired fragrance and spice are added to simple ground beef.

INGREDIENTS

olive oil, for frying
1 red onion, finely chopped
$^2/_3$ cup hot vegetable stock
2 garlic cloves, grated
one 2.5cm (1in) piece of fresh ginger,
   peeled and grated
pinch of ground cinnamon
675g (1$^1/_2$lb) ground beef
grated zest and juice of 1 orange
one (14oz) 400g can chickpeas,
   drained and rinsed
salt and freshly ground black pepper

METHOD

1 Heat a little olive oil in a large pan over low heat. Add the red onion and sauté for 5 minutes, until soft.

2 Add the garlic, ginger, and ground cinnamon to the onions, and season. Stir in the ground beef and cook for a few minutes until the meat is no longer pink. Add the grated zest and juice of the orange, and stir in the chickpeas.

3 Pour in the hot vegetable stock and bring to the boil. Reduce the heat and simmer gently, stirring occasionally, for about 15 minutes.

GOOD WITH Hot, fluffy rice.

4 servings

prep 10 mins
• cook 20 mins

Patatas bravas

Translated as "fierce potatoes", this is a spicy Spanish tapas dish.

INGREDIENTS

6 tbsp olive oil
1½ lb (675g) all-purpose waxy potatoes,
    peeled and cut into ¾ in (2cm) dice
2 onions, finely chopped
1 tsp crushed hot red pepper flakes
2 tbsp dry sherry
finely grated zest of 1 lemon
4 garlic cloves, finely chopped
half of a 14oz (400g) can diced tomatoes,
    with juices
handful of parsley, chopped
salt and freshly ground black pepper

METHOD

1 Preheat the oven to 400°F (200°C). Heat half the oil in a nonstick frying pan, add the potatoes, and cook, turning frequently, over medium-low heat for 20 minutes or until starting to brown. Add the onions and cook for another 5 minutes.

2 Add the pepper flakes, sherry, lemon zest, and garlic and cook for 2 minutes before adding the tomatoes and parsley. Season with salt and pepper, and cook over medium heat for 10 minutes, stirring occasionally.

3 Stir in the remaining oil, and transfer to a shallow baking dish. Bake for 30 minutes until heated through. Serve hot.

GOOD WITH A crisp green salad or a selection of tapas dishes (try Chorizo with peppers, page 130).

4 servings

**prep 15 mins
• cook 30 mins**

Chorizo with peppers

A Spanish-style snack with robust flavors.

INGREDIENTS
2 tbsp olive oil
2 red bell peppers, seeded and cut
　　into ³⁄₄in (2cm) squares
2 green bell peppers, seeded and cut
　　into ³⁄₄in (2cm) squares
3 garlic cloves, crushed
9–10oz (250–300g) chorizo,
　　cut into ³⁄₄in (2cm) cubes
2 tbsp dry sherry
1 tsp dried oregano
salt and freshly ground black pepper

METHOD
1 Heat the oil in a frying pan, add the peppers, and cook over medium heat, stirring occasionally, for 5 minutes. Add the garlic, chorizo, and sherry, and cook for 5 minutes more.

2 Sprinkle the oregano over the top, season with salt and pepper, and serve.

GOOD WITH Toasted ciabatta or other country-style bread as a quick supper or snack, or with other tapas-style dishes (try Patatas bravas, page 128).

4 servings

prep 10 mins
• cook 10 mins

Potato and horseradish hash

Fantastic for brunch, this recipe is a handy use for leftover potatoes.

INGREDIENTS

1 tbsp olive oil
1 tbsp butter
7 bacon slices (200g), chopped
1lb (450g) leftover boiled potatoes, cut into bite-size pieces
    (about 2$\frac{1}{2}$ cups) or 2 cups leftover mashed potatoes
1 tbsp cream-style white horseradish
8oz (225g) curly-leaf kale, cooked, chopped, and squeezed dry
salt and freshly ground black pepper

METHOD

1 Heat the oil and butter in a large nonstick frying pan over medium heat. When the butter has melted, add the bacon. Cook, stirring occasionally, for 5–6 minutes or until golden and crispy. Stir in the potatoes and horseradish, and season well with salt and pepper.

2 Stir in the kale until well mixed. Cook for a few minutes until lightly golden and a little crispy on the bottom. Serve hot.

GOOD WITH Red cabbage.

4 servings

prep 15 mins
• cook 20 mins

133

Make a basic pastry

This is the most versatile pastry recipe, suitable for both tarts and pies. The quantities here suit most recipes.

1 Sift 8oz (225g) of all-purpose flour into a large bowl, and add a pinch of salt. Cut 4^1/$_2$oz (125g) of butter into small cubes, and add to the flour. For best results, use chilled butter.

2 Rub the butter lightly into the flour using your fingertips, lifting the mixture as you go. The more air you incorporate, the lighter the pastry. Continue rubbing until the mixture resembles breadcrumbs.

3 Add about 2 tablespoons of cold water and use a round-bladed knife to bring the ingredients together. Work gently to bind the flour into the mixture.

4 Gather the pastry into a ball using your fingertips. If it is too dry and crumbly, add a little water until it comes together. Cover the pastry with plastic wrap, and chill in the refrigerator for 30 minutes.

Line a tart pan

Follow these steps to line any size and shape of pan. Use chilled pastry, straight from the refrigerator (see left).

1 Roll out the pastry on a lightly floured surface, to a circle about 2in (5cm) wider than the tart pan. The pastry should be fairly thin.

2 Carefully drape the pastry over a rolling pin and gently lay it over the tart pan, so the pastry hangs over the edge on all sides.

3 Gently ease the pastry into the sides of the pan using your fingertips or knuckles, being careful not to tear it.

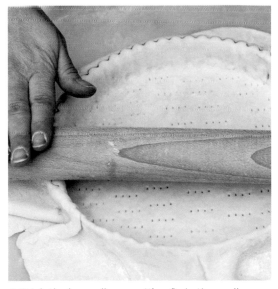

4 Prick the base all over with a fork, then roll a rolling pin over the top of the pan to cut away the excess pastry. Chill for 30 minutes before baking.

Bake pastry blind

A pastry case for a tart or pie must be pre-cooked if its filling will not be baked, or baked only for a short time.

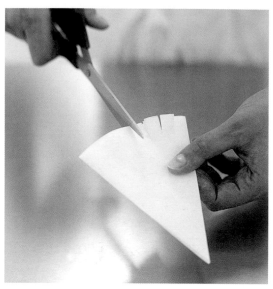

1 Fit the pastry in the pan and ensure that you prick the bottom thoroughly with a fork (see p137). This will allow trapped air to escape during baking and prevent the pastry from rising.

2 Cut out a circle of parchment paper, just slightly larger than the pan. Fold the parchment in half 3 times to make a triangular shape and clip the edge at regular intervals with scissors.

3 Place the parchment circle into the pan and fill it with an even layer of ceramic or metal baking beans. Bake at 350°F (180°C) for 15–20 minutes—it will be partially baked.

4 When cool enough to handle, remove the parchment and beans. Allow to cool slightly before adding the filling and return to the oven to cook fully according to the recipe's instructions.

Decorate and seal pastry

Before baking tarts and pies, remove excess pastry, and decorate the edges for a finished look. For pies, use beaten egg white to seal in moisture.

The forked edge gives an attractive finish and is simple to achieve. Use a fork to press the pastry to the rim of the base. Repeat around the edge of the rim at even intervals.

For a rope edge, pinch the pastry between your thumb and the knuckle of your index finger, then place your thumb in the groove left by the index finger, and pinch as before. Repeat around the edge.

For a fluted edge, push one index finger against the outside edge of the rim and pinch the pastry with the other index finger and thumb to form a ruffle. Repeat around the edge.

To seal a pie, make sure you press the pastry lid firmly to the base. Use beaten egg white to strengthen the seal and to give the top of the pie a glossy finish.

Sausage pie

Sweet, juicy tomatoes are a lovely partner for rich, savory sausage meat.

INGREDIENTS
1 sheet prepared dough for an 8–9in (20–23cm) pie
all-purpose flour, for rolling the dough
1 large egg, lightly beaten
½ tbsp olive oil
1 onion, finely chopped
salt and freshly ground black pepper
1lb (450g) pork sausages, skinned and crumbled
1 tsp dried oregano
4 tomatoes, sliced

METHOD
1 Preheat the oven to 400°F (200°C). Roll out the pastry on a floured work surface, and use to line an 8in (20cm) square baking dish or tart pan. Trim away any excess, line the pastry shell with parchment paper, and fill with baking beans. Bake for 15–20 minutes until the edges are golden. Remove the beans and paper, brush the bottom of the pastry with a little of the beaten egg, and return to the oven for 2–3 minutes to crisp. Remove from the oven and set aside. Reduce the oven to 350°F (180°C).

2 Meanwhile, heat the oil in a large frying pan over low heat. Add the onion and a pinch of salt and cook gently for about 5 minutes until soft. Add the sausage meat, breaking it up with a fork or the back of a fork. Season well with salt and pepper, and sprinkle with the oregano. Cook, stirring frequently, over medium-low heat for about 10 minutes until no longer pink. Leave to cool, then mix in the remaining beaten egg.

3 Spoon the sausage mixture into the pastry shell, then layer the tomatoes over the top. Bake in the oven for 20 minutes until lightly golden. Let cool for 10 minutes, then slice and serve.

GOOD WITH A crisp green salad.

4 servings

**prep 15 mins,
plus cooling
• cook 60 mins**

**8in (20cm) square
fluted pie dish
or tart pan
• baking beans**

Goat cheese tartlets

Oats give the tartlet pastry an interesting texture and flavor that complements the light goat cheese and yogurt filling.

INGREDIENTS
²/₃ cup whole milk
¹/₃ cup Greek-style yogurt
2 large eggs
2 tbsp finely chopped chives
salt and freshly ground black pepper
3oz (85g) crumbled goat cheese

For the oat pastry
³/₄ cup all-purpose flour,
   plus more for rolling the dough
pinch of salt
¹/₄ cup rolled (old-fashioned) oats
4 tbsp cold butter, diced
3–4 tbsp iced water, as needed

METHOD
1 To make the pastry, sift the flour and salt into a bowl. Stir in the oats. Add the butter and rub it in with your fingertips until the mixture looks like coarse bread crumbs. Stir in enough of the water for the dough to hold together. Gather into a disk, wrap in plastic wrap, and refrigerate for 30 minutes.

2 Have ready four 4in (10cm) tart pans with removable bottoms. Divide the dough into 6 portions, and roll out each on a lightly floured work surface into a ¹/₈in (3mm) thick round. Line each pan with a round, trimming the excess dough. Prick the dough with a fork. Refrigerate for 30 minutes.

3 Preheat the oven to 400°F (200°C). Line each tart pan with parchment paper and fill with baking beans. Bake for 10 minutes. Remove the paper and beans and bake until the crusts are lightly browned, about 5 minutes more. Remove the pans from the oven. Reduce the oven temperature to 350°F (180°C).

4 Whisk the milk, yogurt, eggs, and chives in a large glass measuring cup, and season with salt and pepper. Divide the cheese evenly among the pastry shells, and carefully pour in the milk mixture. Bake for 20–25 minutes, until the filling is lightly set and beginning to brown.

5 Leave to cool slightly, then remove from the tins and serve warm, or at room temperature.

GOOD WITH Salad leaves sprinkled with toasted pine nuts.

PREPARE AHEAD Refrigerate the lined tartlet pans up to 1 day in advance. The baked tartlets can be covered and refrigerated for up to 1 day; serve at room temperature.

4 servings

**prep 25 mins,
plus chilling
• cook 35–40 mins**

**four 4in (10cm)
tartlet pans
with removable
bottoms
• baking beans**

Smoked mackerel and scallion tart

A wholesome, affordable fish, smoked mackerel gives this tart a rich flavor.

INGREDIENTS

1 sheet prepared dough for
an 7–8in (18–20cm) pie
all-purpose flour, for rolling the dough
2 eggs, plus 1 extra yolk, for egg wash
1 tbsp olive oil
1 bunch of scallions, white and green parts,
finely chopped
salt and freshly ground black pepper
2 smoked mackerel fillets,
about 3½oz (100g) each, skinned and flaked
1 cup crème fraîche
handful of parsley, finely chopped
1 bunch of chives, finely chopped

METHOD

1 Preheat the oven to 400°F (200°C). Roll out the pastry on a floured work surface, and use to line the tart pan. Trim away the excess, line the pastry shell with parchment paper, and fill with baking beans. Bake for 15–20 minutes until the edges are golden. Remove the beans and paper, brush the bottom of the shell with a little of the egg wash, and return to the oven for 2–3 minutes to crisp. Remove from the oven, and set aside. Reduce the oven temperature to 350°F (180°C).

2 Heat the oil in a small frying pan over low heat. Add half of the scallions and a pinch of salt, and cook gently for about 5 minutes. Spoon evenly over the bottom of the pastry shell, along with the remaining uncooked scallions. Scatter the mackerel over the top, and season with plenty of pepper.

3 Mix together the crème fraîche and the 2 eggs. Add the parsley and chives, and season with a little salt. Stir to blend. Carefully pour over the tart filling, then bake for 20–30 minutes until set and golden. Leave to cool for 10 minutes before removing the sides of the pan.

GOOD WITH A fresh tomato and cucumber salad.

4 servings

prep 15 mins
• cook 50 mins

7in (18cm) round
straight-sided
tart pan with
removable bottom
• baking beans

Vegetable samosas

In India, ghee (clarified butter) is used to make these pastries, but oil works just as well.

INGREDIENTS
3 baking potatoes (1lb/450g)
2 cups cauliflower florets
3 tbsp vegetable oil
2 shallots, sliced
1 cup thawed frozen peas
2 tbsp curry powder
2 tbsp chopped cilantro
1 tbsp fresh lemon juice

For the pastry
2½ cups all-purpose flour,
    plus more for rolling the dough
½ tsp salt
6 tbsp vegetable oil, plus more for deep-frying
1 cup warm water, as needed

METHOD

1 To make the pastry, sift the flour and salt into a bowl. Stir in the oil. Gradually stir in the warm water until the dough comes together.

2 Knead the dough on a floured surface until smooth. Wrap in plastic wrap and let stand at room temperature for at least 30 minutes.

3 To make the filling, cook the unpeeled potatoes until tender, about 25 minutes. Drain and cool. Peel and cut into small dice.

4 Cook the cauliflower in a saucepan of lightly salted, boiling water for 2–3 minutes, or until just tender. Drain.

5 Heat the oil in a large, deep frying pan over medium heat. Add the shallots and cook for 3–4 minutes, stirring frequently, until tender. Add the potatoes, cauliflower, peas, curry powder, cilantro, and lemon juice. Reduce the heat to low and cook, stirring occasionally, until heated through, about 3 minutes. Let cool.

6 Divide the dough into 8 equal balls. Roll out each into a 7in (18cm) round. Cut each round in half, one at a time, and shape into a cone, moistening the edges of the cone to seal. Spoon a little of the filling into a cone, moisten the top edge, and press down over the filling to enclose it. Transfer to a wax paper lined baking sheet.

7 Pour in enough oil to come halfway up the sides of a large, heavy saucepan, and heat to 350°F (180°C). In batches, fry the samosas for 3–4 minutes, or until golden brown on both sides. Transfer to paper towels to drain. Serve warm or at room temperature.

GOOD WITH A bowl of chutney or raita.

PREPARE AHEAD The samosas can be prepared 1 day in advance, chilled, and fried just before serving.

makes 16

prep 45 mins, plus resting and cooling
• cook 35–40 mins

large saucepan
• deep-frying thermometer

freeze, uncooked, up to 1 month

Stuffed filo tartlets

A stylish appetizer that is great for entertaining.

INGREDIENTS

6 sheets thawed frozen filo dough
olive oil, as needed
3 red or orange bell peppers, seeded, and cut into quarters
10oz (300g) firm smoked chorizo, sliced
$\frac{1}{2}$ red onion, very finely sliced
5oz (140g) goat cheese, crumbled

METHOD

1 Preheat the oven to 350°F (180°C). Brush 1 filo sheet with oil and cut into quarters. Place a filo quarter in a tartlet pan. Stack the remaining three sheets on top of the first, giving each a quarter turn before stacking. Fold the filo over the edge of the pan. Brush with oil and bake for 10 minutes, until crisp and golden.

2 To make the filling, broil the peppers, skin side up, until the skin is blackened and blistered. Cool. Peel and cut into thick slices.

3 Heat 1 tbsp oil in a frying pan and cook the chorizo until crisp and browned. Drain on paper towels.

4 Arrange the peppers, onion, and cheese on the tarts. Top with hot chorizo to serve.

6 servings

prep 45 mins
• cook 20 mins

six 4in (10cm)
tartlet pans

Empanadas

These savory Spanish pastries make very versatile nibbles.

INGREDIENTS
3¼ cups all-purpose flour
½ tsp salt
6 tbsp cold butter, diced
3 large eggs, beaten
1 tbsp olive oil
1 onion, finely chopped
⅓ cup canned chopped tomatoes, drained
2 tsp tomato paste
one 6oz (175g) can tuna, drained
2 tbsp finely chopped parsley

METHOD
1 To make the pastry, sift the flour and salt into a large mixing bowl. Rub in the butter with your fingertips until it resembles fine bread crumbs. Beat 2 of the eggs with 2 tbsp water, add to the bowl, and stir until the dough holds together. Make a thick disk, cover with plastic wrap, and refrigerate for 30 minutes.

2 Meanwhile, heat the oil in a frying pan over medium heat. Cook the onion, stirring often, for about 5 minutes, or until translucent. Add the tomatoes and tomato paste, and simmer, stirring often, about 10 minutes, until thick. Remove from the heat and stir in the tuna and parsley. Season with salt and pepper.

3 Preheat the oven to 375°F (190°C). Roll out the dough to a thickness of ¹⁄₁₆in (2mm). Cut out 24 rounds with a 3½in (9cm) round cookie cutter. Fill each with a spoonful of the filling. Brush the edges with water, fold over, and press the edges closed with a fork.

4 Place the empanadas on an oiled baking sheet and brush with the remaining egg. Bake for about 15 minutes, or until golden. Serve warm.

6 servings

**prep 45 mins,
plus chilling
• cook 40–50 mins**

**3½in (9cm) round
cookie cutter**

Cheese and onion tart

Anchovies give a salty kick to this mildly flavored onion tart.

INGREDIENTS

$\frac{1}{3}$ package refrigerated pie dough
3 tbsp olive oil
1lb (450g) onions, thinly sliced
3oz (85g) farmer's cheese
2 large eggs
$\frac{1}{2}$ cup half and half
1 tsp caraway or cumin seeds, crushed
salt and freshly ground black pepper
one 2oz (60g) can anchovy fillets in oil,
    drained and rinsed

METHOD

1 Roll out the pie dough on a lightly floured work surface, and use to line the tart pan. Chill for 30 minutes.

2 Heat the oil in a large saucepan over low heat. Add the onions and cover. Cook, stirring occasionally, about 20 minutes, until the onions are meltingly tender. Uncover and cook for 4–5 minutes more, or until golden. Let cool.

3 Meanwhile, preheat the oven to 400°F (200°C). Line the tart crust with parchment paper and fill with baking beans. Bake about 10 minutes, until set. Remove the paper and beans and bake until beginning to brown, about 10 minutes more.

4 Reduce the oven temperature to 350°F (180°C). Spread the onions in the shell. Whisk together the cheese, eggs, half and half, and caraway or cumin seeds. Season with salt and pepper and pour over the onions. Arrange the anchovies on top. Bake for 25 minutes, or until the filling is set. Cool slightly then remove the sides of the pan. Serve warm.

PREPARE AHEAD The tart can be baked a few hours in advance then reheated in a 350°F (180°C) oven for 15 minutes, until hot.

4–6 servings

**prep 15 mins,
plus chilling
and cooling
• cook 1 hr 15 mins**

**8in (20cm) tart
pan with
removable bottom
• baking beans**

Cheesy spinach squares

Spanakopita, the Greek spinach pie, can be cut into small diamonds or squares and served as an appetizer.

INGREDIENTS
4 tbsp olive oil
1 onion, peeled and chopped
8 scallions, white and green parts, chopped
2lb (900g) spinach, rinsed and shredded, but not dried
3 tbsp chopped dill
3 tbsp chopped parsley
4 large eggs
8oz (225g) feta cheese, finely crumbled
freshly ground black pepper
10 tbsp butter, melted
14 sheets thawed frozen filo dough

METHOD
1 Heat the olive oil in a large saucepan over medium heat. Add the onion and scallions and cook, stirring occasionally, about 5 minutes, until softened.

2 Stir in the spinach, and cover. Cook, stirring occasionally, about 8 minutes, or until wilted. Stir in the dill and parsley, and increase the heat to medium-high. Cook, uncovered, stirring frequently, for about 15 minutes, until the liquid evaporates and the mixture starts to stick to the bottom of the saucepan. Transfer to a colander lined with paper towels, and let cool.

3 Beat the eggs in a large bowl. Add the spinach and feta cheese and season with plenty of pepper.

4 Preheat the oven to 325°F (160°C). Generously brush the pan with some melted butter. Line the pan with a sheet of filo dough, carefully pressing it into the sides and corners of the pan. Repeat with 6 more filo sheets.

5 Spread the spinach mixture into the pan. Repeat layering and buttering the remaining 7 filo sheets. Using kitchen scissors, trim away excess dough, and tuck the filo edges into the pan. Brush the top with any remaining butter. Bake for 1 hour, or until the pastry is crisp and golden brown all over.

6 Cut into squares and serve hot or warm.

GOOD WITH Other Greek or Middle Eastern appetizers, such as hummus and taramasalata, as a mezze platter.

PREPARE AHEAD The filling can be prepared through step 2, and refrigerated for up to 1 day.

12 servings

prep 35 mins, plus cooling • cook 1 hr 30 mins

11½ x 8in (29 x 20cm) baking or roasting pan

155

Feta and pumpkin pastries

Popular Middle Eastern snacks, these tasty filo pastries are filled with a sweet-savory mixture.

INGREDIENTS

one 4oz (115g) piece pumpkin or winter squash, peeled and seeded
4oz (115g) feta cheese, finely crumbled
3 tbsp chopped raisins
½ tsp ground cinnamon
freshly ground black pepper
8 sheets thawed frozen filo dough
all-purpose flour, for dusting
4 tbsp butter, melted, plus extra for the baking sheet

METHOD

1 Cut the pumpkin flesh into very small dice and place in a small saucepan. Pour in enough water to barely cover, and bring to a boil. Reduce the heat to low, cover, and simmer for 5 minutes, or until tender. Drain and let cool.

2 Preheat the oven to 350°F (180°C). Mix the pumpkin, feta cheese, raisins, and cinnamon, and season with the pepper.

3 Stack the filo sheets on top of each other and cut the stack into 4 long strips, about 3in (7.5cm) wide for a total of 24 strips. Cover the strips with moistened paper towels.

4 Lightly dust a baking sheet with flour. Working with 1 strip at a time, brush the strip with butter. Place a heaping teaspoonful of the pumpkin and cheese mixture about 1in (2.5cm) from the bottom end. Fold over a corner of the strip diagonally to cover the filling and form a triangular pocket of filled pastry. Working upward, keep folding diagonally, from one side to the other, to retain the triangular shape, until all the pastry is folded, making sure any gaps in the pastry are pressed closed. Transfer the triangle to the baking sheet and cover with a damp paper towel. Repeat with the remaining ingredients.

5 Butter another large baking sheet. Arrange the triangles on the buttered sheet. Brush with the remaining melted butter. Bake for about 20 minutes, or until crisp and golden. Serve hot or warm.

GOOD WITH Other Greek or Middle Eastern dishes as part of a mezze selection.

PREPARE AHEAD The pastries can be refrigerated up to 24 hours before baking.

makes 24

prep 20 mins,
plus cooling
• cook 30 mins

Ricotta and bacon tart

A simple, stylish tart with a light but smokey-flavored filling.

INGREDIENTS

1 tbsp butter
1 onion, chopped
4oz (115g) sliced bacon, chopped
1 cup ricotta cheese
2 large eggs
$\frac{1}{3}$ cup whole milk
3 tbsp grated Parmesan cheese
1 tbsp finely chopped chives
1 tbsp finely chopped thyme
salt and freshly ground black pepper

For the pastry

$1\frac{1}{4}$ cups all-purpose flour,
   plus more for rolling the dough
$\frac{1}{4}$ tsp salt
6 tbsp cold butter, diced
4 tbsp iced water, as needed

METHOD

1 Preheat the oven to 400°F (200°C). Make the pastry: Sift the flour and salt into a large bowl. Add the butter and cut into the flour with a pastry blender until it resembles coarse bread crumbs. Stir in enough water to make a firm dough. Wrap and chill for 30 minutes. Roll out on a floured work surface into an $\frac{1}{8}$in (3mm) thick round. Line the tart pan with the pastry and trim any excess. Refrigerate for 30 minutes.

2 Put the pan on a baking sheet. Line the tart shell with parchment paper, fill with baking beans, and bake 15 minutes, until the dough looks set. Remove the paper and beans and bake another 5 minutes, until the pastry starts to brown. Transfer to a wire rack to cool. Reduce the oven to 350°F (180°C).

3 Meanwhile, melt the butter in a frying pan over medium-low heat. Add the onion and cover. Cook, stirring, for 10 minutes, until tender. Add the bacon and increase the heat to medium-high. Cook, uncovered, stirring, about 5 minutes.

4 Meanwhile, mix the ricotta, eggs, and milk. Stir in the Parmesan, chives, and thyme. Season with salt and pepper. Stir in the bacon and onion and pour into the pastry shell. Bake for 35 minutes or until the filling has set. Let cool in the pan. Transfer to a serving platter and serve.

6–8 servings

prep 35 mins, plus chilling • cook 1hr 10 mins

9in (23cm) tart pan • baking beans

freeze for up to 3 months

Gruyère tart

This vegetarian tart has a crisp, thyme-flavored pastry.

INGREDIENTS

1 tbsp butter
1 tbsp olive oil
1 large onion, thinly sliced
1 tsp sugar
pinch of freshly grated nutmeg
1 cup shredded Gruyère cheese
¾ cup half-and-half
3 large eggs
1 tsp Dijon mustard
salt and freshly ground black pepper

For the pastry

1 cup all-purpose flour,
   plus more for rolling the dough
⅓ cup whole wheat flour
9 tbsp cold butter, diced
1 tsp chopped thyme
4–5 tbsp iced water as needed

METHOD

1 To make the dough, stir the flours together. Add the butter and rub it with your fingertips until it resembles coarse bread crumbs. Stir in enough of the water so that the dough holds together. Shape into a thick disk, wrap in plastic wrap, and refrigerate for 30 minutes.

2 On a lightly floured surface, roll the dough into a ⅛in (3mm) round circle and use to line a tart pan with a removable bottom. Prick it lightly all over with a fork. Chill for 30 minutes.

3 Preheat the oven to 400°F (200°C). Line the dough with parchment paper and fill with baking beans. Bake for 10 minutes. Remove the paper and beans and bake for 10 minutes more, until the crust is golden and crisp. Remove from the oven. Reduce the oven temperature to 375°F (190°C).

4 Meanwhile, to make the filling, heat the butter and oil in a large frying pan. Add the onion and cook over low heat, stirring frequently for 15 minutes, until tender. Stir in the sugar and nutmeg and cook for about 3 minutes more, until golden. Transfer to a plate and cool.

5 Stir half the Gruyère cheese into the cooled onion mixture, then spread in the pastry shell. Sprinkle with the remaining cheese. Whisk the half-and-half, eggs, and mustard together and season with salt and pepper. Pour into the shell. Bake for 30 minutes, until lightly set.

6 Let cool on a wire rack for 10 minutes. Remove the sides of the pan and serve warm or cooled.

GOOD WITH An arugula or watercress salad with sliced plum tomatoes and black olives, tossed in a lemon-flavored dressing.

PREPARE AHEAD The pastry, wrapped in plastic wrap, and the onion mixture, stored in an airtight container, can be refrigerated for up to 1 day. Let the dough stand at room temperature for 15 minutes before rolling out.

6 servings

prep 25 mins, plus chilling
• cook 45 mins

14 x 5in (35 x 12cm) tart pan
• baking beans

Olive, thyme, and onion tart

An easy-to-make tart—there is no need to blind bake the pastry case.

INGREDIENTS

3 tbsp olive oil
3 onions, finely sliced
2 tbsp chopped thyme
1 tsp sugar
salt and freshly ground black pepper
1 cup heavy cream
3 large eggs, beaten
¼ cup freshly grated Parmesan cheese
2 tbsp tapenade

For the pastry

8 tbsp butter
3 tbsp milk
1¼ cups all-purpose flour
1 tsp baking powder
¼ tsp salt

METHOD

1 To make the pastry, melt the butter in the milk in a small saucepan over low heat. Stir the flour, baking powder, and salt together. Add to the saucepan and stir until the dough forms a ball. Remove from the heat and cool. Press firmly and evenly into a 9in (23cm) tart pan. Chill for 30 minutes.

2 Preheat the oven to 375°F (190°C). Heat the oil in a frying pan over high heat. Add the onion and cook, stirring often, for about 5 minutes. Add the thyme and sugar, and season with salt and pepper. Reduce the heat to low and cook gently, stirring occasionally, for about 30 minutes, or until onions are very soft and slightly caramelized. Meanwhile, whisk the cream, eggs, and Parmesan together.

3 Place the tart pan on a baking sheet. Spread the tapenade over the pastry bottom. Spread the onions on top of the tapenade and carefully pour in the cream mixture. Bake for 30 minutes, or until the filling is set and browned. Let cool on a wire cake rack. Remove the sides of the pan, slice, and serve warm or cool to room temperature.

GOOD WITH An arugula salad dressed with a nutty vinaigrette.

PREPARE AHEAD The pastry shell can be prepared up to 1 day ahead.

6 servings

**prep 40 mins,
plus chilling
• cook 30 mins**

**9in (23cm) tart
pan with
removable bottom**

163

Parmesan cheese and walnut tart

This nutty pastry works brilliantly with the creamy cheese filling.

INGREDIENTS

1²/₃ cups all-purpose flour,
   plus more for rolling the dough
¹/₃ cup walnuts
9 tbsp cold butter, diced
1¹/₂ cups heavy cream
2 large eggs, plus 2 large egg yolks
1¹/₄ cups grated Parmesan cheese
freshly ground black pepper
pinch of nutmeg
1 tsp chopped rosemary, oregano, or thyme

METHOD

1 Preheat the oven to 400°F (200°C). Pulse the flour and walnuts together in a food processor until the nuts are very finely ground. Add the butter and pulse until it resembles coarse bread crumbs. Sprinkle in 4 tbsp cold water and pulse until it clumps together, adding more water if needed.

2 Roll the pastry on a floured surface into a ¹/₈in (3mm) thick round. Line the tart pan with the dough, trimming any excess. Prick the dough with a fork and refrigerate for 30 minutes.

3 Line the pan with parchment paper and baking beans. Bake for 10 minutes. Remove the paper and beans and bake for 10 minutes more until golden brown. Reduce the oven temperature to 350°F (180°C).

4 Whisk the cream, eggs, and egg yolks together well. Add the cheese and season with the pepper and nutmeg. Pour into the pastry shell and sprinkle with the rosemary. Bake for 25 minutes, until set.

5 Let cool for 10 minutes, then carefully remove the sides of the pan. Slice the tart and serve warm.

GOOD WITH Mixed greens and tomato salad.

PREPARE AHEAD The baked tart can be refrigerated for up to 2 days.

6–8 servings

**prep 25 mins,
plus chilling
and cooling
• cook 45 mins**

**food processor
• 9 x 9in (23 x
23cm) or
14 x 4½ in (35 x
11cm) rectangular
pan with
removable bottom
• baking beans**

**freeze for up to
3 months**

Sausage, bacon, and egg pie

This pie transports well and so is good for picnics.

INGREDIENTS
1lb (450g) bulk pork sausage
1 small onion, finely chopped
1 tbsp whole grain mustard
pinch of freshly ground nutmeg
salt and freshly ground black pepper
6 strips bacon
4 large eggs
milk, to glaze

For the pastry
1³/₄ cups all-purpose flour
12 tbsp cold butter
¹/₄ tsp each salt and pepper
¹/₄ cup iced water, as needed
1¹/₂ tbsp ketchup

METHOD
1 To make the pastry, pulse the flour, butter, salt, and pepper in a food processor until the mixture resembles coarse bread crumbs. Mix the water and ketchup, add to the flour, and pulse until the dough clumps (add more water, if needed). Gather into a disk, wrap in plastic wrap, and refrigerate for 30 minutes.

2 Preheat the oven to 400°F (200°C). Roll out a bit more than half of the dough on a lightly floured surface into a round about ¹/₈in (3mm) thick. Line an 8in (20cm) springform pan with the dough.

3 Mix the sausage, onion, mustard, and nutmeg, then season with salt and pepper. Spread in the pie crust, and top with the bacon. Make 4 indentations in the sausage with the back of a soup spoon. Crack each egg into an indentation. Roll out the remaining dough. Center over the filling, trim the excess dough, and pinch the edges to seal. Score a crosshatch pattern on top and brush with a little milk. Refrigerate for 15 minutes.

4 Bake the pie for 20 minutes. Reduce the oven to 350°F (180°C), and bake for 30 minutes, until golden brown. Cool the pie before serving.

PREPARE AHEAD The pastry dough can be wrapped in plastic wrap and refrigerated up to 1 day ahead.

6–8 servings

**prep 15 mins,
plus chilling
• cook 50 mins**

**food processor
• 8in (20cm)
springform pan or
tart pan with
removable bottom**

Steak and ale pie

Beer helps to tenderize the beef and imparts a delicious flavor.

INGREDIENTS

1½lb (675g) beef chuck, trimmed and cut
    into ¾in (2cm) pieces
salt and freshly ground black pepper
3 tbsp all-purpose flour,
    plus more for rolling the dough
3 tbsp vegetable oil
1 large onion, chopped
4oz (115g) white mushrooms, halved
1 garlic clove, minced

¾ cup beef stock
¾ cup dark ale
1 tbsp Worcestershire sauce
1 tbsp tomato paste
½ tsp dried thyme
1 bay leaf
1 sheet thawed frozen puff pastry
1 large egg, beaten, to glaze

METHOD

1 Season the beef with salt and pepper. Toss in the flour and shake off the excess.

2 Heat 2 tbsp of the oil in a large nonstick frying pan over medium-high heat. In batches, add the beef and cook, turning, for 5 minutes until browned. Transfer to a large saucepan.

3 Add the remaining oil to the frying pan. Add the onion and cook over medium heat, stirring, until softened. Add the mushrooms and garlic and cook, stirring, about 5 minutes, until the mushrooms begin to brown. Transfer to the saucepan. Stir in the stock, ale, Worcestershire sauce, tomato paste, thyme, and bay leaf into the saucepan and bring to a boil. Reduce the heat to medium-low, cover, and simmer about 1½ hours, or until the meat is tender.

4 Transfer the meat and vegetables to the pie dish. Reserve ⅔ cup of the sauce, and pour the rest over the meat mixture. Let cool.

5 Preheat the oven to 400°F (200°C). Roll out the puff pastry on a floured surface to a thickness of ⅛in (3mm). Cut an 11in (28cm) round. Cut ¾in (2cm) strips from the trimmings. Brush the rim of the pie dish with water, and place the strips around it. Brush with water. Place the pastry round over the dish and press the pastry edges together to seal. Trim off the excess with a knife.

6 Crimp the pastry edge and use the pastry trimmings to make decorations, if desired. Brush the pastry with beaten egg, make a hole in the middle, and affix the decorations on the pastry, if using. Place the dish on a baking sheet. Bake for 25 minutes, or until the pastry is puffed and dark golden. Serve immediately, with the reheated reserved sauce passed on the side.

PREPARE AHEAD The filling can be cooked, cooled, and covered 1 day ahead.

4 servings

**prep 20 mins,
plus cooling
• cook 2 hrs
15 mins**

**9in (23cm)
pie dish**

Squash and Gorgonzola tart

This works well with either creamy Gorgonzola dolce, or the firmer, sharper piccante variety.

INGREDIENTS

1lb (450g) butternut squash,
  peeled and seeded
olive oil, as needed
14oz (400g) baby spinach
2 large eggs, plus 1 large egg yolk
1¼ cups heavy cream
⅛ cup freshly grated Parmesan cheese
½ tsp freshly grated nutmeg
salt and freshly ground black pepper
4oz (115g) Gorgonzola cheese, crumbled

For the pastry

1½ cups all-purpose flour
8 tbsp cold butter, diced
4 tbsp iced water, as needed

METHOD

1 For the dough, pulse the flour, butter, and ¼ tsp salt in a food processor until the mixture resembles coarse bread crumbs. Add the water and pulse until the dough comes together, adding more water if needed. Shape into a thick disk and wrap in plastic wrap. Refrigerate for 30 minutes. Roll out into a round about ⅛in (3mm) thick. Use the dough to line an 8in (20cm) fluted tart pan with a removable bottom. Chill for 30 minutes.

2 Preheat the oven to 400°F (200°C). Prick the bottom of the pastry shell. Line it with parchment paper and fill with baking beans. Bake about 15 minutes, until the dough looks set. Lift off the parchment paper and beans. Bake for 10 minutes more, until beginning to brown. Transfer to a wire rack.

3 Slice the squash into thick slices and spread on a baking sheet. Toss with 1 tbsp oil. Bake for 30 minutes, or until tender. Meanwhile, cook the spinach with 2 tbsp olive oil in a covered saucepan for about 4 minutes, until wilted. Drain and let cool. Whisk the eggs, egg yolk, cream, Parmesan cheese, and nutmeg together and season to taste with salt and pepper.

4 Squeeze the spinach dry. Spread it in the pastry shell, and top with the squash and Gorgonzola. Pour in the custard. Bake for about 30 minutes, or until the custard is set. Let cool for 10 minutes. Remove the sides of the pan and serve hot.

6 servings

**prep 25 mins,
plus chilling
and cooling
• cook 1 hr 30 mins**

**food
processor
• 8in (20cm)
tart pan
• baking beans**

**freeze unbaked
pastry shell for
up to 1 month**

171

Steak and kidney pudding

A classic old English recipe that is just the dish for hearty appetites.

INGREDIENTS

1½lb (675g) round steak
7oz (200g) beef kidney, trimmed
3 tbsp all-purpose flour
salt and freshly ground pepper
1 onion, chopped
6oz (175g) button mushrooms, quartered
2 tbsp Worcestershire sauce
¾ cup plus 2 tbsp beef stock, cold, as needed

For the pastry

1⅔ cups self-rising flour
½ tsp salt
5½oz (150g) suet or lard, shredded
¼ cup iced water, as needed

METHOD

1 To make the pastry, sift the flour and salt into a bowl. Stir in the suet. Make a well in the center. Stir in just enough iced water to mix to a soft, but not sticky, dough. Shape into a thick disk, wrap in plastic wrap, and refrigerate.

2 To make the filling, trim the excess fat from the steak. Cut the meat and kidney into bite-sized pieces. Season the flour with salt and pepper then toss the steak and kidney pieces in the flour to coat evenly. Mix with the onion and mushrooms.

3 Roll out two-thirds of the pastry. Line a 6-cup oven-proof bowl with the pastry, letting the excess hang over the side. Add the meat mixture, packing it snugly in the bowl, taking care not to tear the pastry. Sprinkle in the Worcestershire sauce, and add just enough stock to cover three-quarters of the filling.

4 Roll out the remaining pastry to make a lid. Brush the overhanging edge of the pastry with cold water. Place the lid on top, and press the two layers of pastry together to seal. Flute the edges.

5 Cut a circle of parchment paper larger than the top of the bowl. Pleat the top, to create surplus paper that will allow the pudding to expand. Secure on top of the bowl. Cover this with a double layer of pleated aluminum foil. Firmly crimp the foil around the rim of the bowl to secure it, or tie with kitchen string.

6 Place the bowl on a steamer rack, or on an upturned saucer, in a large stockpot. Add boiling water to almost reach the bottom of the bowl. Cook at a brisk simmer, adding more boiling water as needed as the water evaporates, for 4 hours, or until the crust is firm. To serve, remove the foil and paper. Run a knife around the edge of the pudding to loosen, then turn out on to a serving plate.

GOOD WITH A selection of winter vegetables, such as carrots, cabbage, or leeks.

PREPARE AHEAD The pastry can be made up to 1 day in advance, wrapped and refrigerated until needed.

6–8 servings

prep 30 mins
• cook 4 hrs

6-cup
oven–proof bowl

freeze for up to
3 months

Leek and cheese tart

Also known in France as *flamiche*, this savory puff pastry tart can be served for brunch, lunch, or supper.

INGREDIENTS

3 tbsp butter
2 large leeks, white and pale green parts only,
　halved lengthwise, cleaned, and thinly sliced
6oz (175g) cream cheese, at room temperature
¼ cup freshly grated Parmesan cheese
¼ cup heavy cream
2 tbsp finely chopped chives
large pinch of freshly grated nutmeg
salt and freshly ground black pepper
one 17.3oz (490g) box thawed frozen puff pastry
1 egg yolk, beaten

METHOD

1 Preheat the oven to 400°F (200°C). Line a large baking sheet with parchment paper.

2 Melt the butter in a medium frying pan over medium-low heat. Add the leeks, cover, and cook, stirring occasionally, for 15 minutes or until tender. Cool.

3 Mix the cream cheese, Parmesan, cream, chives, and nutmeg together in a bowl. Stir into the leeks and season with salt and pepper.

4 On a lightly floured work surface, roll 1 pastry sheet into a 12 x 9in (30 x 20cm) rectangle, then trim 1in (2.5cm) from the short side. Place on the lined baking sheet. Spread the filling over the pastry, leaving a ¾in (2cm) border. Brush the border with the beaten yolk. Roll and trim the remaining pastry to the same size. Center over the filling, and seal the edges with a fork. Refrigerate for 10 minutes. Brush the top with the egg yolk. Using the tip of a knife, pierce a few slits in the center of the tart. Score the top in a criss-cross pattern. Bake for 30 minutes, until golden brown. Let cool for 10 minutes, then slice and serve.

GOOD WITH Mixed greens or a tomato and onion salad.

PREPARE AHEAD The baked tart can be made up to 2 days in advance, covered in plastic wrap, and refrigerated.

6 servings

**prep 30 mins,
plus chilling
and cooling
• cook 45 mins**

**freeze for
up to 1 month**

Cheese and pepper jalousie

Quick to make, this pastry makes the most of ready-prepared ingredients.

INGREDIENTS
one 17.3oz (490g) box thawed frozen puff pastry
all-purpose flour, for rolling the dough
3 tbsp sun-dried tomato paste
1 cup shredded sharp Cheddar cheese
one 10oz (300g) jar sliced roasted peppers, drained
4oz (115g) mozzarella, thinly sliced
freshly ground black pepper
beaten egg or milk, to glaze

METHOD
1 Preheat the oven to 425°F (220°C). Dampen a large baking sheet. Roll out one sheet of the pastry on a lightly floured surface. Trim into a 10 x 6in (30 x 15cm) rectangle. Place the pastry on the baking sheet. Roll out and trim the remaining pastry to a 10 x 7in (30 x 18cm) rectangle. Lightly dust it with flour, then fold in half lengthwise. Make cuts ½in (1cm) apart along the folded edge to within 1in (2.5cm) of the outer edge; unfold.

2 Spread the tomato paste over the pastry on the baking tray, leaving a 1in (2.5cm) border. Top with the Cheddar. Pat the pepper slices dry with paper towels, then arrange them on the Cheddar cheese. Sprinkle with the mozzarella and season with pepper.

3 Brush the edges of the pastry with water. Carefully place the remaining pastry over the filling and press the edges together to seal, trimming excess pastry. Brush with beaten egg. Bake for 25 minutes, or until golden brown and crisp. Let cool for 5 minutes, then slice and serve.

GOOD WITH A green salad.

4 servings

prep 20 mins
• cook 25 mins

Sweet corn and pepper filo triangles

Filo, popular for its crispness and flakiness, is perfect for these vegetable-stuffed triangles.

INGREDIENTS

1 tbsp olive oil
1 onion, finely chopped
salt and freshly ground black pepper
3 red bell peppers, seeded and diced
one 12oz (350g) can whole kernel corn, drained
6oz (175g) feta cheese, crumbled or cut into
    small cubes (about 1½ cups)
7oz (200g) thawed frozen filo dough
melted butter, plus more for glazing

METHOD

1 Preheat the oven to 400°F (200°C). Heat the oil in a frying pan over low heat. Add the onion and a pinch of salt, and cook gently for 5 minutes until soft and translucent. Stir in the peppers, and continue cooking for 10 minutes until the peppers are soft. Stir in the corn and feta, and season with pepper.

2 Lay out the filo sheets in four stacks of 3 or 4 layers about 12 x 4in (30 x 10cm), brushing each layer with a little melted butter. Divide the corn mixture between each stack of pastry, spooning it on to the bottom right-hand corner of each one. Fold this corner so that it forms a triangle and encloses the filling, then fold down the top right-hand corner. Repeat until you have made 5 folds in all for each one—similar to folding a flag—and end up with 4 large triangles.

3 Brush the triangles all over with a little melted butter, and place on an oiled baking sheet. Bake in the oven for about 20 minutes until crisp and golden. Serve hot.

GOOD WITH A green salad.

makes 4

prep 20 mins
• cook 20 mins

freeze for up to
3 months

Feta filo pie

Crisp pastry encases a delicious blend of spinach, feta, and pine nuts in this classic Middle Eastern dish.

INGREDIENTS

2lb (900g) spinach, rinsed
4 tbsp butter
2 red onions, finely chopped
1 tsp ground cumin
1 tsp ground coriander
1 tsp ground cinnamon
$1/3$ cup finely chopped dried apricots
$1/2$ cup toasted pine nuts
salt and freshly ground black pepper
6 sheets thawed frozen filo dough
10oz (300g) feta cheese, crumbled
parsley sprigs, to garnish
strips of lemon zest, to garnish

METHOD

1 Rinse the spinach leaves, shake off the excess water, and pack into a large saucepan. Cover and cook over medium heat for 8–10 minutes, turning occasionally, until just wilted. Drain well in a colander, pressing the spinach to extract as much water as possible. Let cool in the colander.

2 Meanwhile, melt 2 tbsp butter in a large skillet over low heat. Add the onion and spices and cook 7–8 minutes, stirring occasionally, until softened but not browned. Stir in the apricots and pine nuts and set aside to cool. Preheat the oven to 400°F (200°C).

3 To assemble the pie, melt the remaining butter. Lightly brush an 8in (20cm) springform pan with melted butter. Line the pan with a filo sheet, letting the edges hang over the edge, and brush with butter. Repeat with 5 more sheets, brushing with butter each time and letting the excess hang over.

4 Blot the cooled spinach with paper towels, then chop finely. Stir into the cooked onion mixture, and season with salt and pepper. Spread half of the spinach into the filo-lined pan. Sprinkle with the feta, then cover with the remaining spinach mixture.

5 Piece by piece, fold the overhanging filo over the spinach, brushing with butter as you go. Brush the top with any remaining butter and place the pan on a baking sheet. Bake for 35–40 minutes, until crisp and golden. Let stand for 10 minutes, then carefully remove the sides of the pan.

6 Serve hot or warm, cut into wedges, and garnish with parsley and strips of lemon zest.

GOOD WITH A crisp salad or a selection of seasonal vegetables.

6 servings

prep 30 mins,
plus cooling
and standing
• cook 1 hr

8in (20cm)
springform pan

DESSERTS

Make crêpes

Making great crêpes involves two essentials—the right temperature and the perfect batter. See p212 for ingredient quantities.

1 Heat a little oil or clarified butter in a crêpe pan, or nonstick frying pan, and pour off any excess. Holding the pan at an angle, pour in a little of the batter.

2 Tilt and swirl the pan as you pour in more batter to coat the base of the pan thinly and evenly. Allow to cook gently until the surface starts to bubble.

3 Use a long spatula to loosen the crêpe. It should be a pale gold color underneath. Flip the crêpe back into the pan to cook the other side.

4 Cook until the second side is golden. Place on parchment paper with a layer between each finished crêpe. Continue cooking the rest of the batter.

Make crumble

Adding a crumble to fresh fruit makes a quick dessert. Make sure the butter is chilled and your hands are cool. See p202 for ingredient quantities.

1 Rub unsalted butter into all-purpose flour until it resembles chunky breadcrumbs. Add sugar and oats and mix together.

2 Cut fresh fruit to line the bottom of an oven-proof dish. Spoon over the crumble mixture, and bake until golden and crisp.

Core and peel apples

Choose apples that are sweet-smelling, firm, and unbruised. The skin should be taut and unbroken.

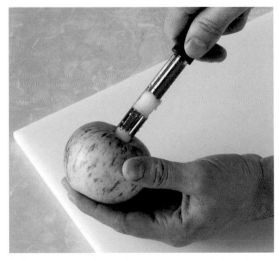

1 Core an apple by pushing a corer straight into the stalk of the apple and through to the bottom. Twist and loosen the core, then pull it out with the corer.

2 Using a peeler or small paring knife, gently remove the skin of the apple by making a circular path around the body from top to bottom.

185

Blueberry cobbler

An old-fashioned summer dessert.

INGREDIENTS

4 ripe peaches, peeled, pitted, and sliced
1lb (450g) blueberries
$\frac{1}{4}$ cup sugar
grated zest of $\frac{1}{2}$ lemon

For the topping

$1\frac{2}{3}$ cups all-purpose flour
$\frac{1}{3}$ cup plus 1 tbsp sugar
2 tsp baking powder
5 tbsp cold butter, diced,
   plus more for greasing the baking dish
pinch of salt
$\frac{1}{2}$ cup buttermilk
1 large egg
3 tbsp sliced almonds

METHOD

1 Preheat the oven to 375°F (190°C). Butter an $11\frac{1}{2}$ x 8in (29 x 20cm) baking dish. Combine the peaches, blueberries, sugar, and lemon zest in the dish.

2 Sift the flour, $\frac{1}{3}$ cup of the sugar, baking powder, and salt into a bowl. Add the butter and rub it in with your fingertips until the mixture resembles coarse bread crumbs.

3 Beat the buttermilk and egg together. Stir into the flour mixture to make a soft, sticky dough. Drop walnut-sized spoonfuls of the dough over the fruit, leaving a little space between each one. Sprinkle with the almonds and 1 tbsp sugar.

4 Bake for 30 minutes, or until the topping is golden brown and the juices are bubbling and a wooden toothpick inserted into the topping comes out clean. Let cool briefly before serving.

GOOD WITH Whipped cream or ice cream.

4 servings

prep 15 mins
• cook 30 mins

Apple Charlotte

This British hot fruit dessert was created for Queen Charlotte.

INGREDIENTS

3lb (1.35kg) Golden Delicious apples,
   peeled, cored, and sliced
1/2 cup plus 3 tbsp sugar
1/2 cup golden raisins
grated zest and juice of 1 lemon
10 tbsp butter, melted
one 1lb (450g) loaf white sandwich bread, unsliced
1/2 tsp ground cinnamon
confectioner's sugar, for garnish

METHOD

1 Combine the apples, 1/2 cup of the sugar, raisins, and lemon zest and juice in a heavy saucepan. Cover and cook over low heat for 8–10 minutes, shaking the pan occasionally, until the apples are very tender and beginning to fall apart.

2 Preheat the oven to 375°F (190°C). Brush the inside of the pan with some of the butter. Remove the crusts from the bread, then cut the bread into 14 slices. Brush both sides of each bread slice with butter. Mix together the remaining sugar and the cinnamon and sprinkle over one side of the bread.

3 Place 3 slices of bread, sugared side down, in the bottom of the pan, trimming to fit. Cut 8 slices in half, and slightly overlap them, sugared side out, to line the sides of the pan.

4 Spoon the apple mixture into the bread shell. Cover with the remaining bread slices, sugared side up, trimming to fit as necessary. Fold over the bread slices on the side of the pan to slightly overlap the top of the Charlotte. Bake 30–35 minutes, or until crisp and golden. Let stand for 5 minutes, then remove the sides of the pan. Sprinkle with confectioner's sugar and serve warm.

6–8 servings

**prep 30 mins
• cook 40 mins**

**9in (23cm)
springform pan**

Tarte Tatin

This French classic is an upside-down apple tart.

INGREDIENTS

10 tbsp butter, softened
1 cup sugar
6 Granny Smith apples, peeled, cored, and chopped

For the pastry

10 tbsp butter, at room temperature
¼ cup sugar
2 cups all-purpose flour, plus more for rolling the dough
1 large egg, beaten

METHOD

1 To make the pastry, cream together the butter and sugar until light and creamy. Gradually mix in the flour. Stir in the beaten egg and mix just until the dough comes together. Turn the mixture on to a lightly floured surface and knead a few times until smooth. Wrap in plastic wrap, and refrigerate for at least one hour and up to 24 hours.

2 Preheat the oven to 425°F (220°C). For the topping, melt the butter in a 12in (30cm) oven-proof frying pan or flame-proof shallow round baking dish over medium heat. Stir in the sugar. Increase the heat to medium-high and cook, stirring often, for 5 minutes, or until the mixture is bubbling and light brown. Remove from the heat.

3 Arrange the apples, rounded sides down, tightly packed together, in the pan.

4 Roll out the pastry into a round just large enough to fit over the top of the apples. Arrange the pastry on top of the fruit and tuck the edges into the pan. Bake for 30 minutes, or until the pastry is lightly browned. Let cool for 10 minutes. Heat the pan briefly over medium heat, shaking it gently to be sure that the apples aren't sticking to the skillet. Hold a round platter over the pan. Using pot holders, holding the pan and platter together, invert them to unmold the tart. Serve warm.

GOOD WITH A spoonful of whipped cream, crème fraîche, or ice cream.

PREPARE AHEAD You can make the pastry up to 1 day in advance, wrapped and refrigerated.

6–8 servings

prep 30 mins,
plus chilling
• cook 35 mins

12in (30cm)
oven-proof pan
or flame-proof
shallow round dish

Bread and butter pudding

Slow baking will produce a pudding with a smooth, velvety texture.

INGREDIENTS
2 tbsp butter, plus more for the pan
5 slices day-old white sandwich bread
$\frac{1}{3}$ cup raisins
3 large eggs
$1\frac{1}{4}$ cups whole milk
$\frac{3}{4}$ cup half-and-half
$\frac{1}{3}$ cup sugar
1 tsp pure vanilla extract
$\frac{1}{4}$ cup apricot preserves
2 tsp fresh lemon juice

METHOD
1 Lightly butter an 8in (20cm) square baking dish. Butter one side of each bread slice. Cut each slice in half diagonally, and then again.

2 Sprinkle the raisins on the bottom of the baking dish. Top with overlapping bread slices, buttered sides down. Beat together the eggs, milk, half-and-half, sugar, and vanilla. Pour over the bread and let stand for at least 30 minutes.

3 Preheat the oven to 350°F (180°C). Place the dish in a roasting pan and add enough water to reach 1in (2.5cm) up the sides of the baking dish. Bake 30–40 minutes, until the center is barely set.

4 Meanwhile, bring the preserves, lemon juice, and 1 tbsp water to a boil in a small saucepan over medium heat. Strain. Brush the mixture over the top of the pudding. Let stand 5 minutes, then serve hot.

PREPARE AHEAD The pudding can be refrigerated for up to 2 days and served cold, or reheated in a microwave oven.

4 servings

prep 15 mins, plus soaking
• cook 40 mins

Hot chocolate cakes

A treat for all chocoholics. These simple-to-make cakes are baked briefly so that a light sponge surrounds a rich, creamy chocolate center.

INGREDIENTS

9oz (250g) bittersweet chocolate, chopped
3 tbsp butter, softened, plus more for the custard cups
$\frac{2}{3}$ cup sugar
4 large eggs
$\frac{1}{2}$ tsp pure vanilla extract
$\frac{1}{3}$ cup all-purpose flour
pinch of salt

METHOD

1 Preheat the oven to 400°F (200°C). Generously butter the inside of six 6oz (175ml) custard cups, and line each with a round of wax paper. Butter the paper.

2 Melt the chocolate in a heat-proof bowl set over, but not in, a saucepan of simmering water. Remove from the heat.

3 Beat the butter and sugar in a bowl with an electric mixer on high speed for about 3 minutes, until light and fluffy. Beat in the eggs one at a time, beating well after each addition, then add the vanilla. Sift the flour and salt together and stir into the batter, then stir in the chocolate. Divide the batter among the cups. Place the cups on a baking sheet.

4 Bake for 12–15 minutes, or until the sides are set but the centers are still soft. Top each cup with a serving plate. Protecting your hands with a kitchen towel, invert both to unmold the cake. Remove the wax paper. Serve hot.

GOOD WITH A dollop of softly whipped cream or hot custard sauce flavored with grated orange zest.

PREPARE AHEAD The cakes can be prepared through step 3 and stored at room temperature for up to 2 hours.

6 servings

prep 10 mins
• cook 20 mins

six 6oz (175ml)
custard cups
or ramekins
• electric mixer

Sticky toffee and banana pudding

Gooey and delicious, this couldn't be faster to make; use ripe bananas for the best flavor.

INGREDIENTS

1 cup heavy cream
8 tbsp butter
$^2/_3$ cup packed light brown sugar
$^1/_3$ cup maple syrup
6 slices store-bought gingerbread cake
2 large bananas, sliced
$^1/_2$ cup chopped pecans

METHOD

1 Preheat the oven to 375°F (190°C). Combine the cream, butter, sugar, and maple syrup in a small pan and heat gently, stirring constantly until smooth and melted.

2 Layer the cake and bananas in a 9in (23cm) baking dish. Pour the sauce on top and sprinkle with the pecans.

3 Bake for 10 minutes, or until the sauce is bubbling. Serve hot.

GOOD WITH Whipped cream or vanilla ice cream.

PREPARE AHEAD You can assemble the pudding several hours in advance. Toss the bananas in lemon juice first and tuck them under the cake—this will keep them from going brown. Add the toffee sauce and pecans and bake just before serving.

6 servings

**prep 5 mins
• cook 10 mins**

**9in (23cm)
square
baking dish**

Rice pudding

Starchy Italian rice gives this dish extra creaminess.

INGREDIENTS

¼ cup short-grain rice for risotto, such as Arborio
2½ cups whole milk
3 tbsp sugar
1 tbsp butter, plus more for the dish
pinch of ground cinnamon or
    freshly grated nutmeg

METHOD

1 Lightly grease the dish with butter. Rinse the rice under cold running water, then drain well. Combine the rice and the milk in a bowl and let stand for 30 minutes.

2 Preheat the oven to 300°F (150°C). Stir the sugar into the rice. Pour into the dish, dot with butter, and sprinkle with cinnamon. Bake for 2–2½ hours, or until the top is golden.

GOOD WITH A spoonful of berry jam or fruit purée or a scoop of vanilla ice cream.

4 servings

prep 15 mins,
plus resting
• cook 2–2½ hours

1 quart (1 liter)
baking dish

198

Semolina

This milk pudding is warm and comforting.

INGREDIENTS

2 cups whole milk
$\frac{1}{2}$ cup heavy cream
$\frac{2}{3}$ cup semolina (pasta flour)
$\frac{1}{3}$ cup plus 1 tbsp sugar
3 tbsp rose water
4 tsp raspberry jam, to serve
1 tbsp boiling water

METHOD

1 Bring the milk and cream to a boil over medium heat in a medium saucepan. Whisk in the semolina in a steady stream, then the sugar. Bring to a boil then reduce the heat. Simmer, whisking often, for 3–4 minutes, until very thick.

2 Remove from the heat. Whisk in the rose water. If desired, thin the pudding with more milk.

3 Divide among 4 dessert cups. Mix the jam with the boiling water and drizzle over each pudding. Serve warm.

4 servings

prep 5 mins
• cook 15 mins

Plum crumble

A popular, quick, and easy dessert—great for family lunches.

INGREDIENTS

1lb 5oz (600g) plums, halved and pitted
maple syrup or honey, to drizzle

For the topping

1 cup all-purpose flour
7 tbsp cold butter, diced
$\frac{1}{3}$ cup packed light brown sugar
$\frac{2}{3}$ cup rolled (old-fashioned) oats

METHOD

1 Preheat the oven to 400°F (200°C). To make the topping, combine the flour and butter in a large mixing bowl and rub in the butter with your fingertips until the mixture is combined. Work in the sugar and oats. The mixture should remain lumpy.

2 Spread the plums in an oven-proof dish and drizzle with the maple syrup or honey. Crumble the topping over the plums. Bake for 30–40 minutes, or until the top is golden brown and the juices are bubbling.

PREPARE AHEAD The topping can be frozen for up to 1 month. The assembled dish can be frozen for up to 2 months.

4 servings

prep 10 mins
• cook 30–40 mins

**freeze for up to
2 months**

Bananas flambéed with Calvados

Alcohol can boost and blend flavors, as shown in this simple dessert of bananas, citrus, and apple brandy.

INGREDIENTS

2 oranges
4 ripe bananas
4 tbsp unsalted butter
$\frac{1}{2}$ cup packed light brown sugar
2 tbsp lime juice
3 tbsp Calvados, applejack, or brandy

METHOD

1 Remove the zest from half an orange with a potato peeler and mince the zest. Squeeze the juice from both oranges—you should have about $\frac{1}{2}$ cup.

2 Peel the bananas and halve lengthwise. Melt 3 tbsp of the butter in a large nonstick frying pan over medium-high heat. Add the banana and cook until lightly browned on both sides. Transfer to a plate, cover, and keep warm.

3 Add the remaining butter to the pan and melt. Sprinkle in the sugar and cook, stirring occasionally. Add the orange juice and zest and lime juice, bring to a boil, and cook until thickened, about 2–3 minutes.

4 Add the Calvados. Light with a long-handled match and cook until the flames burn out. Return the bananas to the pan and turn gently in the sauce to reheat.

GOOD WITH Vanilla or coconut ice cream, perhaps garnished with toasted coconut shavings and wedges of lime for a more elaborate dessert.

4 servings

prep 10 mins
• cook 10 mins

Pear gratin

A sophisticated, simple, and foolproof dessert.

INGREDIENTS
4 ripe Comice pears
6oz (175g) blackberries
½ cup coarsely chopped walnuts
8oz (225g) mascarpone
2 tbsp dark brown sugar

METHOD

1 Position a broiler rack 6in (15cm) from the source of heat and preheat the broiler. Quarter the pears and remove the cores. Place skin side down in a flame-proof serving dish. Sprinkle with the blackberries and walnuts. Drop spoonfuls of mascarpone cheese over the pears and sprinkle with the brown sugar.

2 Broil for 3–5 minutes, or until the mascarpone is bubbly and sugar begins to caramelize. Serve warm.

GOOD WITH Crisp, buttery cookies.

4 servings

prep 10 mins
• cook 3–5 mins

shallow
flame-proof dish

Kaiserschmarrn

Legend says that this Austrian pancake was created for Emperor Franz Josef. Roughly translated as "Emperor's mishmash," it is warming and delicious.

INGREDIENTS
$^2/_3$ cup all-purpose flour
4 large eggs, separated, at room temperature
$^1/_4$ cup plus 4 tsp sugar
$^2/_3$ cup whole milk
2 tbsp butter
$^1/_4$ cup raisins
confectioner's sugar, for serving

METHOD
1 Whisk the flour, egg yolks, $^1/_4$ cup granulated sugar, and milk together in a bowl with a clean whisk until smooth. Beat the egg whites in a separate bowl until stiff peaks form. Fold into the batter.

2 Melt $1^1/_2$ tsp of the butter in an 8in (20cm) nonstick frying pan over medium heat. Pour in one-fourth of the batter and sprinkle with 1 tbsp raisins. Cook 1 minute, until the underside is browned. Turn the pancake and brown the other side. Transfer to a plate. Repeat with the remaining butter, batter, and raisins.

3 Tear the pancakes into pieces using 2 forks. Return the pancake pieces to the frying pan (or a larger one, if you have it) and sprinkle with the remaining sugar. Cook over medium heat about 1 minute, until piping hot.

4 Sift confectioner's sugar on top and serve immediately.

GOOD WITH Plum preserves, the traditional accompaniment. You could also serve with apple preserves or fruit compote, if you don't have plum preserves to hand.

4 servings

prep 10 mins
• cook 10 mins

Spiced plum compote

At their best in late summer to early autumn, plums are perfect for cooking.

INGREDIENTS

1lb (450g) ripe red plums
1 orange
$\frac{1}{3}$ cup sugar
1 star anise
$\frac{1}{2}$ cinnamon stick

METHOD

1 Cut the plums in half and remove the pits. Remove the zest from the orange with a vegetable peeler. Squeeze the juice.

2 Combine the sugar, $1\frac{1}{4}$ cups water, orange zest and juice, star anise, and cinnamon stick in a medium saucepan. Bring to a simmer over medium heat, stirring to dissolve the sugar.

3 Add the plums and stir gently. Reduce the heat to low and simmer for 8–15 minutes until the plums are tender, but still hold their shape. Discard the star anise, cinnamon stick, and orange zest and serve, warm or chilled, in dessert cups.

GOOD WITH Greek yogurt and clear honey.

PREPARE AHEAD Can be made up to 2 days in advance. Keep chilled.

4 servings

**prep 15 mins
• cook 15–20 mins**

Lemon and sugar crêpes

In Paris, these wafer-thin crêpes with the simplest of flavorings are sold by street vendors.

INGREDIENTS
1 cup whole milk
²/₃ cup all-purpose flour
2 large eggs
1 tsp vegetable oil, plus more for cooking crêpes
pinch of salt
lemon wedges and slices and superfine sugar, to serve

METHOD
1 Process the milk, flour, eggs, oil, and salt in a food processor until smooth. Let stand for 30 minutes.

2 Preheat the oven to 200°F (95°C). Heat an 8in (20cm) crêpe or nonstick frying pan, over high heat until a splash of water "dances" on the surface. Pour in enough vegetable oil to cover the bottom, swirl the pan to coat, then pour off the excess oil.

3 Ladle about 3 tbsp of the batter into the center of the pan and immediately tilt and swirl the pan so the batter covers the base thinly. Cook the crêpe for about 1 minute until small bubbles appear on the top. Slide a metal spatula underneath and flip the crêpe over, then continue cooking for 30 seconds more, or until golden and cooked through.

4 Transfer to a plate, roll up, and keep warm in the oven. Repeat, oiling the pan as needed, until all of the batter has been used. Serve the crêpes hot, sprinkled with sugar, drizzled with lemon juice, and served with lemon slices.

GOOD WITH A drizzle of maple syrup, or fruit purée in addition to the lemon and sugar. These pancakes can also be enjoyed with a whole range of fillings such as stewed fruit or sliced bananas.

PREPARE AHEAD Make the crêpes in advance, and layer with wax paper, then wrap in plastic wrap. Reheat in the oven before topping with lemon juice and sugar.

4 servings

prep 15 mins,
plus standing
• cook 10 mins

food processor
• 8in (20cm)
crêpe pan

freeze the crêpes,
separated by
waxed paper, for
up to 3 months

Baked jam roll

This English pudding was traditionally steamed, but baking makes the crust crisper. You can use any jam, but raspberry works particularly well.

INGREDIENTS

1²/₃ cups all-purpose flour,
    plus more for rolling the dough
1¹/₂ tsp baking powder
¹/₄ tsp salt
8 tbsp cold butter,
    shredded on a box grater
¹/₂ cup whole milk
¹/₃ cup jam, any flavor
1 large egg, beaten
sugar, for sprinkling

METHOD

1 Preheat the oven to 400°F (200°C). Line a baking sheet with wax paper.

2 Sift the flour, baking powder, and salt into a bowl. Mix in the butter. Stir in the milk to make a stiff dough. Roll on a lightly floured work surface into a 10 x 7in (25 x 18cm) rectangle.

3 Spread the dough with the jam. Starting from a long side, roll into a log. Lift and transfer the roll to the baking sheet, seam side down. Lightly brush with the beaten egg and sprinkle with the sugar.

4 Bake for about 25 minutes, or until golden brown and crisp.

GOOD WITH Custard sauce, warm crème anglaise, or whipped cream.

4–6 servings

prep 10 mins
• cook 30 mins

Torrijas

In Spain, this version of French toast is usually served as an indulgent pudding rather than as a breakfast dish.

INGREDIENTS
8 slices stale baguette, crusts removed
$3\frac{1}{4}$ cups whole milk
3 tbsp granulated sugar
1 cinnamon stick
1 cup olive oil, for frying
3 large eggs, beaten
confectioner's sugar, for sifting
maple syrup, for drizzling

METHOD
1 Arrange the bread in a shallow dish. Bring the milk, sugar, and cinnamon to a boil in a saucepan, stirring often, over medium heat. Pour over the bread. Let stand for 15 minutes, until the bread has soaked up all the milk. Remove the cinnamon stick and discard.

2 Preheat the oven to 200°F (95°C). Line a baking sheet with paper towels. Heat the oil in a large frying pan over medium heat until the oil shimmers. Beat the eggs in a shallow dish. In batches, dip a slice of the bread in beaten egg to coat, then add to the frying pan. Fry, turning once, until golden. Transfer to the paper towels and keep warm in the oven.

3 Transfer to a serving platter, sift the confectioner's sugar on top, and drizzle with syrup. Serve the slices while still warm.

4 servings

prep 5 mins, plus standing • cook 20 mins

Hot orange soufflés

Hot soufflés are not difficult to make, but they do need a little care. This is a basic sweet soufflé, flavored with orange zest.

INGREDIENTS

4 tbsp butter
⅓ cup sugar, plus more for the ramekins
⅓ cup all-purpose flour
1¼ cups whole milk
grated zest of 2 oranges
2 tbsp fresh orange juice
3 large eggs, separated, plus 1 large egg white

METHOD

1 Preheat the oven to 400°F (200°C). Place a baking sheet in the oven to preheat.

2 Melt the butter in a medium saucepan over medium heat. Brush six 7oz (200ml) ramekins with some of the butter. Dust the insides of the ramekins with sugar, making sure there are no gaps.

3 Whisk the flour into the remaining butter and let bubble over medium heat without browning for about 1 minute. Whisk in the milk and bring to a boil, whisking constantly. Reduce the heat to low and simmer for 2 minutes. Whisk in the orange zest and juice and all but 1 tsp of the sugar.

4 Remove from the heat and beat in the egg yolks one at a time. Whisk the whites to soft peaks, then beat in the remaining sugar. Stir a dollop of the whites into the saucepan, then fold in the remainder.

5 Divide among the ramekins. Using a knife, make a shallow circle around the ramekins about ¼in (6mm) in from the edge. Place on the hot baking sheet and bake for 15 minutes, or until the soufflés have risen but look slightly unset in the center. Serve immediately.

4 servings

**prep 20 mins
• cook 12–15 mins**

6 ramekins

**freeze, uncooked,
in the ramekins
for up to 1 month**

Quindim

This sweet, creamy, and very rich dessert is a popular party dish in Brazil.

INGREDIENTS

melted butter, for the ramekins
$\frac{1}{2}$ cup sugar, plus more for the ramekins
4 large egg yolks
$\frac{1}{4}$ cup canned coconut milk
2 tbsp desiccated coconut
grated fresh coconut, toasted, to serve

METHOD

1 Preheat the oven to 350°F (180°C). Butter the insides of four 4oz (120ml) ramekins and coat with sugar, tapping out the excess.

2 Whisk the sugar and egg yolks until light and creamy. Add the coconut milk and desiccated coconut; mix well. Divide among the ramekins. Place the ramekins in a roasting pan and add enough hot water to come halfway up the sides.

3 Bake for about 25 minutes, until set. Remove from the pan and cool briefly. Run a knife around the inside of each ramekin to loosen the custard. Invert on to individual dessert plates. Refrigerate until chilled, about 3 hours. Serve chilled.

PREPARE AHEAD The quindim can be refrigerated for up to 1 day before serving.

4 servings

**prep 15 mins,
plus chilling
• cook 25–30 mins**

**chill for at
least 3 hrs**

4 ramekins

ACKNOWLEDGMENTS

DORLING KINDERSLEY WOULD LIKE TO THANK THE FOLLOWING:

Photographers
Carole Tuff, Tony Cambio, William Shaw, Stuart West, David Munns, David Murray,
Adrian Heapy, Nigel Gibson, Kieran Watson, Roddy Paine, Gavin Sawyer, Ian O'Leary,
Steve Baxter, Martin Brigdale, Francesco Guillamet, Jeff Kauck, William Reavell, Jon Whitaker

Picture Researcher
Emma Shepherd

Proofreader
Anna Osborn

Indexer
Susan Bosanko

Useful information

Refrigerator and freezer storage guidelines

FOOD	REFRIGERATOR	FREEZER
Raw poultry, fish, and meat (small pieces)	2–3 days	3 months
Raw ground beef and poultry	1–3 days	3 months
Cooked whole roasts or whole poultry	2–3 days	9 months
Cooked poultry pieces	2–3 days	3 months
Soups and stocks	2–3 days	3–6 months
Stews	2–3 days	3 months
Pies	2–3 days	3–6 months

Oven temperature equivalents

FAHRENHEIT	CELSIUS	DESCRIPTION
225°F	110°C	Cool
250°F	130°C	Cool
275°F	140°C	Very low
300°F	150°C	Very low
325°F	160°C	Low
350°F	180°C	Moderate
375°F	190°C	Moderately hot
400°F	200°C	Hot
425°F	220°C	Hot
450°F	230°C	Very hot
475°F	240°C	Very hot